Dr. Memsaab

Stories of a Medical Missionary Mom

PHYLLIS IRWIN, M.D.

AuthorHouse™
1663 Liberty Drive
Bloomington, IN 47403
www.authorhouse.com
Phone: 1-800-839-8640

First published by AuthorHouse   6/18/2010

ISBN: 978-1-4520-2540-7 (e)
ISBN: 978-1-4520-2538-4 (sc)
ISBN: 978-1-4520-2539-1 (hc)

Library of Congress Control Number: 2010907182

Printed in the United States of America
Bloomington, Indiana

This book is printed on acid-free paper.

Contents

Preface

FRONTIER CHALLENGE

I enjoy the mountains, the grandeur of the scenery and the challenge of getting to a destination, but I do not particularly like the climb. For many years we lived in the foothills of the Himalayas, in the Northwest Frontier Province of Pakistan. Many times we have climbed mountain paths to reach the village of someone we wanted to visit, or to minister medically. Sometimes we climbed for fun with the children when they were home from boarding school, and we would go off to some rest house. But the physical challenge of climbing in the Himalayas is nothing compared to the challenge of Islam, which shares so much with Christianity and yet is so different.

God has always challenged his people to do things that are difficult or impossible for man, in order to show his power, and how weak we are in ourselves. Moses was challenged to lead his people out of Egypt. Against all odds, God showed his power through mighty miracles. Joshua was told to go up against Jericho, which was impossible for mere men, but God demonstrated his power and victory was won. Many times Ezekiel prophesied the defeat of Israel's enemies so that "…then the nations will know that I am the Lord…" Ezekiel 36:23 In smaller ways, God challenges all of us to attempt things for him which we are unable to do in ourselves, so that the Glory may be his.

When my husband Russ and I were called to go half a world away from our humble rural roots in Indiana, and attempt to bring the Gospel to the Muslim people in the Northwest Frontier of Pakistan, we felt we had no strength or training to meet that challenge, except the Lord do it through us. Who were we, just simple country folk who had never been abroad, to challenge the entrenched religion of that area? The stories in this book are glimpses and examples of how God worked out his plan for us and accomplished what he wished, through his power.

There is nothing spectacular in our story, no overwhelming spiritual victories with whole peoples turning to Christ, no network of indigenous convert churches established. There are just some insights, as to how God worked in our own lives and a few others with whom we have crossed paths. Yes, a small rural hospital was established, many nationals trained, a Bible Institute established, a family raised. But the real work done has been in our own lives to conform us more into the image of the Lord Jesus.

The meaning of Doctor Memsaab

"Saab", a contraction for Sahib, is a term used in British-ruled India for British officers and others of important rank. The prefix "Mem" , contracted from Madam, was added when used for the wives of "saabs." I was known as "Doctor Memsaab" by patients, staff and friends during our thirty-five years at Bach Christian Hospital in northern Pakistan.

From letters, memory, and diaries the story is woven of our life together during 39 years our Lord allowed us to serve Him in Pakistan. Our last four years were spent in Lahore, 250 miles south of Bach Christian Hospital.

Phyllis Irwin, M.D.

The Seasons Of My Life

SPRING began for me when I was born in 1928 in New Albany, Indiana, as the youngest of three. I grew up in the small village of Milltown, near the Ohio River. I had a happy childhood with parents who loved each other and the Lord. I had two older brothers who challenged me to learn to skate, ride a bike, and swim in the river that ran through our town. We were active in our small town church. We were poor, but did not realize it—everyone was poor during those years of depression in the 30's. My father was an auto mechanic and worked 60 hours a week to support his family. The early spring of my life was very happy, of which I have only joyful memories. It was not until many years later that I realized that a solid family was a marvelous gift of God. I was especially aware of this when I saw the damage in those from dysfunctional families. WWII took my two brothers4 off to the Air Force and Navy. My older brother did not return, bringing the first big tragedy in my life. He was the pilot of a B-24 bomber and was shot down over France on his 30th mission. He was 21. This had a profound effect on me and caused me to think of eternal values. The Lord brought me into a personal experience of salvation just before my senior year of high school—the old fashioned way by going to the altar at a revival meeting. That spiritual event changed my life and gave me a focus.

I went to Asbury College where I was awed by the big world that opened up to me. My small town environment hedged in my world. At college I heard missionaries who opened up the whole world of need and opportunities to serve Jesus in other cultures. I was challenged to career missionary service. There was no such thing as short term missions back then. When I committed my life to be a missionary, there was no turning back. I never again considered anything else. This included my willingness to go single. When I surrendered even this to the Lord, He gave me real peace and joy. I changed my major to pre-med and applied to medical schools in my senior year. In those days not many women entered medicine. I was one of four females in my class of 150, even though applications flooded in from post-war vets on the GI Bill.

During my freshman year of medical school on the Bloomington campus, I met Russ Irwin through Inter Varsity Christian Fellowship. I made sure on our first date that he was planning on being a missionary—or there would not have been a second date! He delights in telling how I "popped the question" on our first date! We were married after our sophomore years in medical school and seminary. We graduated from our respective schools in 1954.

My year of internship took us to a hospital in Riverside, CA. While there, Russ worked in the x-ray department and also pastored a small church. During those years, the Lord led step by step to a mission board, TEAM, and to a Muslim field, West Pakistan. By the time we were back in Indianapolis for my Obstetrics and Gynecology residency, we were pretty well set for overseas. Then his draft board informed him that if we intended to go abroad as missionaries, we had better go, as his number was coming up, and they had no more valid exemptions for him.

Some people questioned why we would go half way around the world to some wild place with a baby, when we could have successful careers here in comfortable America. Jesus said in Matthew 16:25, "If you try to keep your life for yourself, you will lose it. But if you give up for life for me, you will find true life." In 1956 we sailed for West Pakistan with our year-old daughter Patty. Somewhere on that voyage my spring changed to summer! Josh 1:9 was the verse the Lord gave me as we started on the unknown. "Fear not, neither be thou dismayed, for I the Lord thy God am with thee whithersoever thou goest."

SUMMER: These were busy years, roughly from age 28 to 45. They were productive years. We helped build a hospital in the Northwest Frontier of West Pakistan, raised a family of three, developed a hospital staff, and treated many thousands of patients annually. Our son Nate was born the day before I had my first year language test (I think the test initiated labor!). I delivered him on a dining room table without anesthesia during a monsoon rainstorm in a mountain town in the Himalayas, attended by a lady missionary physician. Since no vehicular traffic was available, she arrived by horse just in time!

I started work at the hospital as soon as my written Urdu tests were done 2 weeks later. Our younger daughter was born in relatively posh facilities back in USA on our first furlough. Now I was challenged with the task of being a Mom with three kids, wife, missionary, medical superintendent and chief staff physician of a 50-bed hospital. The days were sometimes not long enough to get everything done. I absolutely loved medicine, and although I worked many 12⁺ hour days for many years, I was fascinated by the variety of pathology and far advanced conditions that confronted us every clinic day. I was moved with compassion by the desperate needs of these poor Muslim patients. In those days and up in our area a male doctor could not see women patients. As word spread that there was a lady doctor at Bach Christian Hospital, patients came from many miles around, especially from the mountains to the north. Some traveled days to reach the hospital.

We saw hopeless, far advanced TB of lung, TB of the spine, bone and joints, nodes, even kidney and skin. There were also horrid childbirth injuries, neglected fractures requiring amputation, disfiguring burn scars, parasitic infections, malnutrition of the worst degree in children, and the dreaded diarrheal diseases that takes so many lives of babies and children. Complicated labor cases began coming. A lot of this I had never seen before; so we struggled and learned from reading books.

We improvised, and prayed. We saw lots of extensive burns requiring skin grafting. We did hernias, bladder and urethral stones, drained huge TB abscesses containing quarts of caseous pus. There were lots of Caesarian Sections, even more tubal ligations, and lots of osteomyelitis operations to remove dead bone. The Lord's hand was in every healing, and it was amazing that in an almost 100% Muslim area, we were able to tell these people about Jesus. We prayed with every patient before surgery in the name of Jesus. We distributed Bibles and literature freely, although the literacy rate, especially among women, was very low. A few responded - most did not - but all respected us and our Christian message.

Meanwhile, the children were growing up, enjoying playing on the compound with Pakistani and expatriate staff children. I was always amazed at how little it took to entertain them. No TV, no videos or computers, no organized activities at the Y or church because there weren't any! Simple walks to the stream, picnics nearby, trips to the river to swim, and table games in the evenings kept them happy. As pre-schoolers, our ayah, or nanny, cared for them. She was dear Safedie, a Pakistani lady from a nearby village who was with us for many years. She loved the kids, and they loved her.

We took the children with us on treks for clinics in the "boonies" back in the mountains. The kids watched surgery; the girls saw deliveries, and when they were older, actually worked in the hospital as "aides" during vacations from boarding school. We were prepared for boarding school before we came, so there was no decision about that.

Regarding boarding school there was no other option. It was hard to say good-bye, but so joyous to see them come home for breaks! Boarding school was a positive experience for all our kids, which I know is not true for all MK's. This was another gift of God's grace to us. That may be part of why all three kids became missionaries themselves. The following verse often comes to mind: 3 John 4: "I have no greater joy than to hear that my children are walking in the truth."

LET'S SEE, I was also a wife. When was there time for that? The Lord gave me a very wonderful, spiritual, flexible, genial husband who was a great father when I often wasn't there for the kids. In the early years he did about every job in the hospital except doctoring. He was building and maintenance-in-charge, as well as administrator, and chaplain. He set up our x-ray unit and taught the lab tech how to take and develop x-rays. He always had time for people, spending much time in counseling. He was gone a lot on hospital business, committee meetings, preaching, teaching Bible courses. We had to plan carefully to do things as a family when the kids had time at home. I know there were times when Russ felt I was too busy and urged me to slow down. I never figured out how to do it, when up to 200 or more people daily were thronging the gates for medical help. A great love for each other, from the Lord himself, helped us get through that summer season of life with rejoicing. Mark 1:33, "... the people brought....all the sick and demon possessed."

FALL: FALL ALREADY! This is roughly age 45 for the next 22 years. Before we knew it, Patty was ready to go to the USA for college, followed by Nate a year later. Thank goodness we had Cindy for four more years! Those good-byes were harder than boarding ones! Transportation and finances were better by then, and we were able to get to the USA for graduations and weddings. I think the hardest good-bye for me was when Patty was eight months pregnant with our first grandchild as we returned to the field. Communication was not what it is now, and it took a few days to get a telegram telling us that we were grandparents. It took even longer to get a phone call through to talk to her to find out the reason she had to have a "Sea Section," as the telegram stated. Now we can direct dial, and exchange emails daily!

Before many years, the children were coming back, this time as adults and career missionaries themselves! Patty and Carl went to the Philippines, and we would visit them on the way to and from the USA. Nate, and then Cindy, came to Pakistan with our same mission. None went into the medical field, but followed in their dad's footsteps. What a joy to work with them as fellow missionaries! Nate was Principal of our Bible Institute, training Christian Pakistanis for ministry, until they had to return to the USA for Nate's inner ear problem. Cindy has had an exciting ministry with Afghan women refugees, teaching ESL. Many have become believers in Christ from their very strong Muslim background. This was not at the school, but through social contacts and visits outside of school hours. Whole families come for Bible Study and discipling with hardly time to schedule them all! Patty and family after seven years were asked to return to the US for Carl to become one of the mission directors at the headquarters of C&MA in Colorado Springs.

With more adequate hospital staff, Russ was now relieved of a lot of his hospital jobs, and was able to do more Bible teaching. He was director of the Bible Correspondence Course for some years, helped found the Bible Institute of which our son was principal, and helped initiate the Theological Education by Extension program in Pakistan. He wrote programmed courses for this, and taught teachers to teach it.

At the hospital, we were developing training programs in several areas. Two doctors initiated a Community Health program, training village health workers. About 50,000 outpatients were being seen annually, 1500 babies delivered, and over 2000 surgical procedures done. We trained young Christian Pakistani men and women to be nurses' aides, and some of the girls went on to learn midwifery. We trained lab techs, x-ray techs, and physiotherapy aides. We had medical students from the western world for 2-3 months at a time on rotation, and medical and surgical residents from the Aga Khan medical school in Karachi rotate through for 3 months at a time. I was privileged to train nurses to be "clinic screeners" (nurse practitioners) both for the hospital and outlying clinics.

A young Christian Pakistani doctor came to us right out of medical school, so he had the equivalent of internship with me. He learned to see clinic patients efficiently, do minor surgery and even Cesarean Sections. For several years we were the only 2 doctors. Later he started developing his own mission clinic farther to the north, with a vision to get Pakistani Christians involved in reaching out to Muslims. Even a couple of Bible women have been trained to fill the ranks of the older ones retiring. They talk to the women, and make follow up visits in homes. Our staff is now almost completely Pakistani from Administrator and Nursing Superintendent to doctors and nurses to gardeners. The spiritual emphasis has been maintained, so that patients and their relatives are exposed to the Gospel daily. It is with great praise that we have seen the hospital services and training programs continue after we left. The spiritual emphasis has been maintained, so that patients and their relatives are exposed to the Gospel daily.

Again I say, "I have no greater joy than to hear that my children are walking in the truth."

WINTER: So NOW it is winter! We retired from Pakistan in 1995 at age 67, leaving a daughter Cindy, son Nate and wife Marty, and 3 of our grandchildren in Pakistan. We returned to the old farmhouse where Russ's grandparents had lived when he was a child.

So how does one spend the winter years? No, I am NOT doing any medical practice! So many people have asked that! It is unrealistic for a post retirement age physician who has practiced 39 years overseas to enter the jungle of highly specialized, technical, managed care medicine we have today. I am used to having my own hospital where we write the rules, set the fees, and patient care is entirely in the hands of the doctor! I happily relinquish 40 years of night call and 12 hour days! We have more time together as a couple than we ever had before. I am a Teetotaler, but they tell me wine is better when it is aged, and so it is with our marriage! It gets better and better!

What keeps us busy? We have had a lot of remodeling and fixing up to do with the old farmhouse. That is mostly Russ's department. I enjoy a big garden, and we have an orchard of apples and pears, and one cherry tree. Summers are busy canning, freezing and giving away produce. I am trying to organize and summarize my journals of 60 years into something readable. We are active in two of our churches. We keep busy in doing prison and sick visitation and in various speaking engagements. We have time to attend conferences and seem to be on the road a great deal. Email correspondence takes a daily hunk of time. We have been able to renew contact with many old friends and relatives, attend reunions and enjoy things we have not been able to do for many years. I highly recommend the retirement, or winter years! Of course, we also have to deal with the inconveniences of aging. But we are really quite healthy for this decade of the 70's, and thank God daily for that.

What lies ahead? We don't know how much it is going to snow this winter, as we are just starting this season of our lives. As for any season of life, God holds the plan, so we know it is good. If it includes sickness, loss, death and disappointment, we trust God to prepare us for that and bring blessing through it. Our children and grandchildren bring us much joy, our friends and relatives are a source of strength and happiness, and we are blessed. Blessed be the name of the Lord! Psalm 92:12-15

2

Voyage To Pakistan - 1956

We traveled tourist class on the Christoforo Colombo, which meant a tiny stateroom way down in the bowels of the ship, which was about the size of some dressing closets in the States. We were on "second sitting" to eat in the dining room, which was after 8 PM. This was past Patty's bedtime, but she was a trooper and her ready smile made lots of friends. How many one year olds can claim to have had their first birthday in the mid Atlantic? She had a happy time, opening 3 presents. Two from Ted and Beulah Peterson, who had driven us to the ship in New York, and one that came air mail special delivery to the dock, from Sally Thomas. She was thrilled with her new toys: a cuddly kitty, a pink horse, and a tin tea set, which she banged with great delight! I had to wash out her diapers in the tiny sink in the corner of our stateroom, and drape them around the cabin. But the excitement of exploring the big ship, watching schools of porpoises playing in the waves, making new friends, and having a daily chapel service enlivened our journey. The ship docked at Gibraltar for a few hours, where the Pietsches, who were traveling with us, disembarked to go across the Mediterranean to visit Bill's brother in Tangier. They would rejoin us as we changed ships in Naples.

As our ship neared the dock at Naples, Italy, people on shore cheered and looked for their relatives coming down the gangplank, welcoming them with outstretched arms. I realized that NO ONE was there eagerly waiting for us! We had our first pangs of homesickness! The bustle of disembarking soon dispelled those feelings, and replaced them with the excitement of seeing a foreign land!

We took baby Patty, her suitcases of bottles, formula, and paper diapers (a new product then!) to the hotel Terminus. I attempted to explain to hotel staff that I wanted the bottles boiled, but was met with only puzzled stares! They did not understand English and although they wanted to please me, they could not figure out what I was trying to get them to do! Our next cultural encounter was at the train station as we attempted to board for a sight seeing trip up to Switzerland during the two weeks before we were to get our next ship for Pakistan. We could not figure how to get on the train with our luggage and a baby in the midst of the swirling crowds using loud Italian which we could not understand. We couldn't ask questions, even if someone had been willing to listen! A helpful porter through gestures indicated we should board, and he would hand our luggage in to us through the window! This actually worked, and we were on our way to Rome!

There in the hotel Esperia, our firstborn took her first steps! First birthday in mid Atlantic, first steps in Rome! For four days we took in the famous sights of Rome, including Sunday at St. Peter's in Vatican City. Then on to Switzerland for a delightful few days, and to Frankfurt where we visited some CEF and YFC missionaries. On the way back to Naples we had a day in Venice. We experienced this strange city of water streets by taking a motor launch down the Grand Canal, seeing many gondolas.

Phyllis Irwin, M.D.

We embarked on October 1 on the SS Asia for our destination, Pakistan! On this leg of the trip, Patty improved her gait by walking on the swaying deck! She even tried to run away from me at times! Russ went to the finals in a ping-pong tournament! The Asia was a smaller ship—only 460 passengers, and more friendly. We had much more room in our cabin. Passengers included Americans, English, Scandinavians, Italians, German, Chinese, and many Indians. There were a good number of missionaries, from US, Norway, Denmark, Germany and Canada. A group of us met every morning for Bible study and prayer. There were many children on board, and Patty enjoyed playing with the mostly Indian children in the supervised playroom. The swimming pool was an interesting experience, as the water is so salty (sea water) one cannot sink! Floating was an effortless joy.

We went ashore in Port Said, before we entered the Suez Canal, so we could say we had been in Egypt! There were hawkers every 2 or 3 feet, pushing their wares in our faces, or trying to get us into a horse carriage taxi, or tempt us inside a store, or offering to guide us around. They also swarmed on board the ship and set up shop, while some bargained from little boats alongside the ship.

October 12, 1956. Karachi, Pakistan

We finally arrived in the land of Pakistan, after our years of anticipation and preparation. Praise the Lord! We docked at 2 PM, and by 10 PM Russ and Bill got our stuff through customs, at reasonable rates. We paid about $100. That is, all but the box of Best Locks for the hospital, and the Volkswagen. It was another month before the van came in, and Russ had to return to Karachi to get it cleared and drive up country. We were royally cared for in Karachi by some friends of the Pietsches who were with the American Embassy. They had a big, luxurious home with air conditioning and American food! We went to a Methodist Church to the English service (they also have an Urdu service), and found out the pastor is a fellow Asburian! Russ, Patty, and I also visited the family of Dr. Safia Qadir, the lady doctor we met in Indianapolis. They were very charming, and served us a fancy tea.

We had many first impressions: the great contrast between the very rich and very poor; the camel drawn carts, donkey wagons, the big refugee camps still existing from the partition of India and Pakistan in 1946, with thousands living in the utmost squalor. They wash clothes in mud holes—we saw them doing this right in the middle of the street. They also take baths in these mud holes, urinate and defecate right out in the open, and have herds of water buffalo and goats living right with them in their little straw and rag shelters. So many beggars! Even mothers with babes at breast are begging.

We traveled up country by train—two hot days and a night, leaving Bill to try to get the box of locks cleared, and obtain some forms for the VW. I remember one beggar who put his face up to the window of our compartment to show the hideous cancer that had eaten half of his features away. I quickly turned Patty the other way so she wouldn't see. At the first train stop, there was his face again—he had gotten on the train somehow, and was repeating his performance! In our compartment besides Karen and son Dan, we met another missionary couple traveling to Murree Christian School - Don and Evelyn Calderwood. They were taking baseball bats and gloves, and other sports equipment for the students. They were on the school staff until Patty and her two siblings had graduated from High School!

Never will I forget our welcome as our train pulled into the station in Haripur. The Pietsches were getting off here, and almost the entire mission family had gathered on the platform to welcome us! These folks had prayed for us, corresponded with us, and now at last they welcomed us to our Pakistan TEAM family! A couple of ladies—Ruth Arvidson and Agnes Davis, got on the train with us and rode the last few miles upcountry to the terminus of Havelian. The others drove their vehicles from Haripur to Havelian and were there to welcome us again! The train goes no farther, as the foothills of the Himalayas rise rather quickly to 4,000 ft., the elevation of our destination of Abbottabad. Those final few miles we were driven in the bright moonlight, with breathtaking views of the hills and valleys. At one curve the sparkling lights of Abbottabad appeared as a jewel--our new home was in sight!

Phyllis Irwin, M.D.

3

Letters Home Our First Year--1956-57

November 14, 1956.

While I am typing this on our verandah, Patty is busy with her box of toys. Daddy is inside with our language teacher. We take turns caring for her while the other has class. She doesn't seem much like a baby anymore. She roams all over the place and will never stay in our two rooms if a door is open. She prefers the outside and will go with anyone who offers to take her—or go by herself if she can open the door! She has acquired a fourth jaw tooth, and is chewing all kinds of food. I haven't even used the baby food I brought along, since she prefers table food. Food here is good, if limited in variety. Cauliflower is less than two cents a pound, and we have spinach, carrots, and squash. Buffalo meat is not very tender but costs only about ten cents a pound. We have bananas, guavas, pomegranates, apples, and oranges.

Everything seems to be done differently here. Corn is hand cut, and then oxen tread it out in a little round pit. The grain is then thrown up in the air to let the chaff blow away. A common sight along the roadside is the women and children making dung cakes out of the manure. It is also interesting to watch a road being built. Day after day a group of men sit along the road with small hammers, breaking up the big rocks to make crushed stone, one piece at a time. Only a few have a piece of screen wire over their eyes for protection from the flying chips of rock

We have been having a fire in our little wood stove in the evenings, which sure feels good. We are going to shop for a rug, so our concrete floor won't feel so cold. We have a dresser being made and will order a desk and chair. All furniture is custom made. Show the carpenters a picture in an old catalog, and they make it! Amazing how nice it looks, when all they have are hand tools. We got a handsome little potty chair for Patty. She is quite proud of it and loves to sit on it, although she doesn't know yet what it is for. Sunday she succeeded twice when we put her on at the appropriate time, and she greatly enjoyed our making over her for it!

November 28, 1956

For Thanksgiving we went to the hospital land to visit a missionary couple, where he is directing the building program. Since Thanksgiving is not a holiday here, the dinner was in the evening. We had chicken, dressing, mashed potatoes, carrots, jello salad, pickles, hot rolls apple pie and coffee! There is no electricity at the land yet; so the ice cream was made in a kerosene fridge. We ate by Coleman lantern light. The most interesting part of the day for me, however, was in the afternoon. I was at the clinic, and word came that a woman in a nearby village had been in labor for three days. They refused to bring her to the hospital, as they said she was about to die anyway, and it would cost too much. I suspect the real reason was that they would not bring her to a man doctor (they didn't know I was there for the day.)

A nurse and I set off with a few instruments for the mountain village. The head man (Khan) of the village accompanied us. In fact, he had me ride his horse! About half way there a man came to tell us that the baby had just been born—dead, of course. We decided to go on and see what we could do for the woman. After half an hour journey, we came to this typical village of mud houses, with narrow rocky passageways between the houses and open sewage running down the middle. We came into the courtyard of the patient's house and were met by several weeping women and scores of curious children. They took us into the room where the patient lay, which was a dirty storeroom without windows. The woman was in a corner on the bare floor with only a palm leaf mat beneath her and several dirty blankets on top. With the light of three kerosene lanterns we could barely see her. She was quite weak, exhausted, and infected, but probably would recover with the help of sulfa and iron tablets. I was horrified at the indescribably filthy rag they were using for her pad. I don't see how any of them live, as this is typical of the way they handle maternity cases.

Phyllis Irwin, M.D.

After we treated her, we had to go to the Khan's house for tea. His house is large, with a Kashmiri carpet on the floor. He has been to college, as well as two of his sons. We were served tea and three fried eggs apiece! (Being wealthy, however, does not ensure cleanliness!) This Khan has been quite good to the hospital, helping secure the land, and is now the straw boss of the workers in spite of some severe opposition. He knows the value of medical work for his people. It was after dark when he sent his son back down the mountain with us, with my riding the horse again! We got back just in time for the Thanksgiving supper.

DECEMBER 30, 1956.

We spent a busy Christmas week at Mansehra with Dr. Karsgaard. I went with him to the clinic out at the hospital site every day and saw lots of interesting patients. The new clinic building is still far from finished inside, but better than the old mud quarters in Mansehra. No electricity or running water, nor heat! I nearly froze my feet on the cold concrete floors. I wondered how Pakistani children survive, as I saw them running around barefoot. A little ten-year old girl was brought to the clinic fifteen days after being burned on a leg and chest. Her family had given her the village treatment of plastering her burn with cow dung! Most of these unfortunates die in the village of tetanus or generalized infection; but this girl, with proper treatment, is recovering. She will need a lot of grafting. Another lady who walked several miles to the clinic had vaginal bleeding for eight months. A lab test showed she had only about 20% of a normal blood count. I examined her (she would not let the male doctor do so) and found she has lots of fibroid tumors on her uterus. Unless the relatives will agree to give her blood, she will surely die soon. They probably will not do so, as that sounds like a strange custom to the ignorant villagers. Besides, she is just a woman!

On Christmas Day there was a big feast, or "khana" at the hospital land for the national hospital staff, servants, and their families. The sun shone beautifully; so we ate outside sitting on the rope beds called charpais. We had rice pilao, and hot, spicy curry. For dessert there was yellow sweet rice. The folks loved it, and most of them ate with their fingers. Afterwards, Christmas carols were sung in Urdu, and there was a short message by the evangelist from Mansehra. He is one of the few converted Muslims in our area. Peter is really a wonderful Christian. Christmas night some of the hospital staff came caroling to Dr. Karsgaard's house. They sang to us in Urdu until midnight! The music seems strange, as it is all one part (no harmony) and in a minor strain, sung to the accompaniment of drums and tambourine.

The day after Christmas Russ and I went with Dr. Karsgaard up to the only outlying dispensary we have at the present, just inside the Pakistan-held part of Kashmir. It was a thrilling trip, climbing through the mountains where we had a superb view of the newly covered snowcaps of the Himalayas. It doesn't seem many people live in the area, but on closer inspection, one can see many clusters of mud houses pressed against the sides of the hills. There is a nurse at this dispensary full time, and Dr. Karsgaard visits every two weeks, seeing 60-90 patients each time. There are several women who come into the clinic with the complaint that they have been unable to bear children. They are usually about 18 or 19 years old, and have been married 6 or 7 years! On the way back we saw a jackal, the most common wild animal around here. You can hear them howling almost every night. They sound weird, like a baby crying.

JANUARY 13, 1957.

A prayer request at our monthly day of prayer yesterday was for a young college student, a convert from Islam. He is now being forced by the father into a marriage with a Muslim girl. The father wrote him a threatening letter calling his missionary friends ugly names, and stating that although he had allowed his son quite a bit of freedom, this marriage was absolutely the final word. He had to do it. The boy has a real problem, for going through with the ceremony is tantamount to recanting, and yet the father's pressure on him is great. He told the missionary, "I have to do it, yet I cannot. When I think of my future, I weep." We really can't empathize with these converts, as we haven't had to suffer any persecution for our faith as they have to. Another request is concerning the hospital. A Muslim neighbor of the hospital is bringing a lawsuit, claiming we really aren't there for medical services, but that our main purpose is to make Christians out of the patients! The lawyer on our side is Muslim, but is quite friendly. He tells us that the new constitution guarantees freedom to propagate any religion. I don't think anything will come of the case, but it reflects the attitudes of some of the "enemy."

Phyllis Irwin, M.D.

March 3, 1957

Friday I was at the hospital for women's clinic. Every fourth Friday I will have the clinic alone, with the nurse, as Dr. Karsgaard goes to Lahore to another hospital to do eye surgery. I can't put them through nearly as fast as he can, since I can't speak Urdu well as yet. I don't even know all the new drug names yet (English and German drugs). He saw 100 patients Friday. Saturday I was at the hospital again for six cataract operations, and helped him with a tonsillectomy on one of the school teachers, Rae Steeves, who lives next door to us. A week before I had helped him do a tonsillectomy on his own daughter!

March 17, 1957

Friday I went out to the hospital and saw the women's clinic by myself. It was somewhat rainy; so we didn't have the usual number. I saw about fifty, and it worked much smoother than I had hoped, with our Pakistan lady translator, Mrs. Shah, talking to the women in Punjabi. She would tell the missionary nurse in Urdu, and the nurse would tell me in English! I enjoyed it—good change from language study, and I feel like I am really doing something.

May 3, 1957

We moved to Murree this past week, piling our belongings in a truck along with several other missionaries' stuff. Eight adults, two toddlers, one puppy dog, and the wife of our cook piled in the VW and set off for Murree. We had to go the long way of 120 miles, as the short way across the mountains, only fifty five miles, is still blocked by snow. We had a picnic lunch along the way, much to the amusement of some curious, dirty Pakistani children who watched every move we made! When we left, they eagerly grabbed our lunch papers, tin cans, and even Patty's wet paper diaper, thinking they had some treasure!

Our cottage for the summer is built against the side of the mountain, accessible only by a steep path a couple of hundred yards long. All our stuff had to be carried down by hand. Our water is running only when the man brings it in buckets each morning and dumps it in the water barrel. Our toilets "flush" only twice a day, when the special person who does this work comes and empties the "pots." The house is really nice, though. We have a large living room, a bedroom, a small bathroom of sorts, and share the dining room with the Daltons and two single girls. The communal kitchen is another room across the verandah. I have the job of setting up the kitchen, instructing the cook, Mir Zaman, daily menu planning, market lists, etc. I am also instructing the cook's wife Pearie about the daily washing, cleaning, and taking care of Patty and her playmate Marie Dalton. Tomorrow will be her first day on her own, when we go to language school.

Pearie seems to be bright, and both she and Mir Zaman read and write Urdu. No English, however. He is a convert from Islam. We have daily devotions with them in Urdu, and by next year Russ hopes to take him out into the villages for evangelism. We enjoyed church today in the big, old English garrison church, with missionaries from all over Pakistan. The electricity has not yet been turned on for the summer, and frequently goes off anyway, so we rely on pressure lanterns. It is beautiful up here at 7000 ft., but cool. Anyplace we go is either straight up or down! We sent the VW back to Abbottabad for the summer, as it would be of no use here, and can be used to better advantage there.

May 18, 1957

We are really enjoying language school, held in the union church where we go for services on Sunday. It is about a mile from here, mostly up, and I enjoy the daily exercise. We go from 8:30 to 12:00 and then study on our own in the afternoon, having a private hour or two with one of the teachers. Many of them are Christians and are a real inspiration. One old, lovable, sincere Christian teacher who is going blind, Mr. Rafiq, tells of the real satisfaction he has had teaching hundreds of missionaries their new language for over forty years. Now they are all over Pakistan and India telling people about the Lord.

Pearie handles the washing of our clothes by hand and cleaning with ease, and seems to handle the children all right. Mir Zaman is doing the cooking very well, too. He is a sloppy dishwasher, and we have to keep reminding him to keep things clean, but he is a willing worker. Before we left Abbottabad he asked for a couple of days leave to go see his sick mother. He was gone only about 48 hours, and when he came back, we found out he had walked 23 miles over the mountains to his remote village and 23 miles back. His feet were bruised, and he was limping, but he was smiling and ready to go to work! He says his mother is the only one of his family who still loves him since he became a Christian.

Murree is an interesting place—you either walk, as most do, or take a small two wheeled carriage pulled by men! There are also saddle horses, and mangy little donkeys for the kiddies to ride! The other day Arlene Dalton and I took Marie and Patty for a walk. The man who carries our water lives just below us, and cares for a little gray donkey. His wife put Patty on it and made it go a few steps. Patty was thrilled beyond description. I had to literally drag her away from the place. Now she frequently starts off in that direction, to find her "horsie!"

The Kashmiri coolies here are amazing—these men carry tremendous burdens on their backs up and down the steep hillsides. They can easily carry 300 lbs. on their backs, all day long. That is the cheapest form of transport—one coolie earns about forty cents a day! We have all sorts of "salesmen" come to our door, carrying their goods in huge open baskets on their heads—vegetables, flowers, ivory work, Kashmiri rugs and shawls. They are willing to trade goods for things from America. The Daltons got a nice 4x7 Kashmir rug and three fancy teapot covers for an old Parker 21 pen. In the woods around we have an amazing variety of wild flowers—fern, ivy, waxy yellow buttercups, delicate lavender, columbine, wild pink verbena, pink and white striped wild tulips, and something that resembles lily-of-the-valley. We frequently hear the cuckoo bird, which sounds like the clock of the same name! Russ saw a flying squirrel today. We hear them frequently, as they live between our roof and rafters, making quite a noise scampering about. When Patty hears them, she says "Noise!"

June 20, 1957

It has been hot and dry here for 2 or 3 weeks. The Pakistanis throw their garbage out in the yards, and youngsters squat anywhere outside. The open drainage ditches are beginning to smell. The flies have brought us a small diarrhea epidemic. But the woods are lovely; daisies are thick, and the breezes refreshing. Last weekend we went to Dunga Gali, eighteen miles from here and 2000 ft. higher, to visit the DeHarts who are spending their vacation in a small village there. We had an exciting bus trip over narrow rough mountain roads with no guardrails! A couple of times we almost collided with vehicles coming around a curve, and had to back up to let them pass. Patty and Timmy had a good reunion, celebrating with suckers and balloons from Aunt Kay's packages. Russ and Don climbed a nearby peak and brought snow to make a freezer of delicious homemade ice cream. It is a lovely place, with many mountain paths to follow. We saw our first wild monkey as we were walking along a path to have a picnic.

July 21, 1957

I delivered a baby for a Danish missionary lady who lives downstairs. We did it at a crudely equipped clinic set up for missionaries and staffed by doctors who are here taking turns. The baby is a girl, only 5'4". Patty has been there with me twice when I was checking on the mother and is absolutely thrilled with the "bitty, bitty baby!" She wants one of her own, so I think we will oblige her in a few weeks! I'm sure he won't be that little—I think he is already bigger than that!

August 3, 1957

Mrs. Frello started to develop a breast abscess, and her baby boy has infected ears, so I have been giving penicillin shots every day. The result of which is that last evening Patty sat down with her doll, an empty penicillin bottle, a pencil, and proceeded to give the doll a shot! When she sees me get out my black bag she gets a sorrowful look on her face and says, "Sick!" When we are talking about the coming baby, she will pat my stomach and say, "Get it out!" I am finding it difficult to navigate up the hill to language school—Russ often pushes on my back in the steep places! We will all be glad when baby arrives!

August 27, 1957

I had quite an exciting weekend! I took my oral Urdu finals on Saturday morning, and then did a lot of odd jobs in the afternoon that I had been putting off because of studying. I passed my test with a 90% "Distinctive"—more than I had dreamed of! Saturday night I had a couple of hours of what turned out to be false labor, but enough to get Russ and me up boiling syringes and needles and getting all the equipment ready! Then Sunday I decided to try to start things again, so I took

Phyllis Irwin, M.D.

castor oil and an enema. That worked with Patty! At 5 p.m. contractions started again, but were mild, so I didn't say anything for an hour.

Everyone here in Bexley was tense, standing by waiting for me to produce! We sent for Dr. Bruce at 6:30 p.m. in a rainstorm. She had to come on horseback, and it took her over an hour from the time we sent for her. By that time I desperately needed her, as things were moving fast! We sent for Dr. Bev Feldmann just down the hill, too. Dr. Bruce arrived just as Nathan's head was coming out! No time for any anesthesia (I had planned for a spinal) or even sterile drapes or anything! It wasn't nearly as bad as I had thought it would be. She used local anesthetic to sew me up. The electricity went out as she was doing that, so she finished by flashlight! Such a relief to have 9 lb. 5 oz. Nathan Douglas out where we could see him! All the women in Bexley Cottage were on hand to view his birth. It was the first time for two of them; two others were nurses.

Of course, Russ was on hand and wonderful through it all. Patty woke up and cried, so Russ brought her in to see her brand new brother! She was sleepy, but wide-eyed and smiling when she saw him! I am feeling wonderful—much better than after Patty. Nathan has a good amount of dark hair, a button chin, small mouth, and generous nose.

Oct. 7, 1957

We had an exciting trip down from Murree in our VW with the kids, which was the first time "over the top." It is only forty five miles but takes almost three hours, as it is all mountainous, gravel road, with hair-pin curves and sheer drop offs of 700-800 feet with no guard rails! One 15-mile stretch is so narrow in many places that vehicles can't pass, so there are gates at either end, with timed one-way traffic. This road was closed by snow when we moved to Murree in May. As we looked at the vistas of mountainsides, each terraced to the very top to utilize every parcel of tillable ground, we realized how many thousands are tucked away here, with no Christian witness.

Russ had to return to Murree with a truck to bring down all our belongings. The nurse, Vi Bleeker, and I were the only staff to run the hospital, since the rest were at Annual Conference. I had to take Patty and Nathan along with me to the hospital. Nathan slept nicely in his car bed in Dr. Karsgaard's office, and Patty sat on the examining table and watched me talking to patients! She got a bit weary but did pretty well. The patients enjoyed it, of course. I don't like to have her there at all, because of the many tuberculous patients and other infectious diseases, but I had no choice. When everyone is back, she won't go with me, as there will be plenty of other missionary kids to play with.

When Russ got back with our stuff, he told of the five Kashmiri coolies helpers, who carried such tremendous loads on their back. They carried our stuff up the steep hill from Bexley Cottage to the truck. They are fascinating to watch. One carried our refrigerator on his back; another, our double folding bed. Still others carried heavily loaded 55-gallon oil drums! They wear heavy, padded coats and balance the stuff on their lower backs, lean way over, and sort of waddle along. The load is steadied by ropes, which they hold. Our cook Mir Zaman says he has seen one of them pick up a motorcycle and carry it up Murree's steep hills!

We have an interesting patient, a young girl who has been here for quite a long time. Dr. Karsgaard is trying to get her ready for plastic surgery. Hers is a fairly typical story. She was actually or supposedly unfaithful to her husband, so he tied her to a tree, and in the presence of the entire village, cut off her nose and her left ear! Apparently this happens rather frequently!

Phyllis Irwin, M.D.

Oct. 22, 1957

At last we are writing from our first real home of our own in Pakistan! Leaky, drafty, and cold though it may be, we are finally by ourselves! These quarters will be for Pakistani staff eventually. We have had unseasonably cold weather and steady rains the past three days, and find our new roof leaks in several places! Getting settled has been a bit hectic with my starting to work in the hospital right away. Dr. Karsgaard has been away five days, so I've had all the clinics, rounds, etc. We are getting experience with kerosene irons, pressure lanterns and kerosene heaters. It will be a while before the electrical transformer will be installed so they can then put up the poles, wiring, and meters for the housing. We'll appreciate it when it comes! Mail arrival is rather sporadic—whenever someone happens to bring it out from Abbottabad ten miles away.

Nov. 12, 1957

Nate is getting quite heavy now, and what an appetite! He can eat cereal and an 8 ounce bottle and still act like he wants more! This is every four hours around the clock, or he's famished! He's on the bottle now—I couldn't keep up with him! Pearie isn't with us yet, as the servants' quarters aren't built, and there is no decent place for her to stay. We have a rented room near the hospital for Mir Zaman, but it won't do for a family. I sure need someone, since Russ is so busy in the construction work.

Dec. 8. 1957

The other day I found Patty in her bedroom talking to Aunt Kay's picture, saying "Auntie Kay, suckers lao!" That means, bring the suckers! Yesterday when I was at the hospital for an operation, Patty dipped her little blankie she sleeps with into the diaper pail, got it soaking wet, then crawled up on OUR bed and took a nap! When I got home, things were a mess! The ayah was here, so I had to bawl her out for letting such a thing happen. She gave me a big long explanation, but I couldn't understand much of it!

Russ has made a clever closet in which to hang clothes, out of the packing crate our refrigerator came in! It really helps, as we had no place to hang clothes. He can nicely fix things up when he has time. Maybe he will find more time now that the rainy season is here, when he can't do as much outside. Our roof doesn't leak nearly as much since he improved it.

Dec. 27, 1957

Russ and Earl Parvin worked 12-14 hours a day trying to get electricity by Christmas, and at 9:30 p.m. Dec. 23rd, the lights went on! We were so excited, going around switching on the lights in every room! I had put the two sets of lights on our tree that we had just gotten in a box from home, just in hopes. Now we are enjoying them, even though some of the wires from the main transformer were temporarily lying on the ground. How appreciative we are after three months of kerosene! Christmas Eve we had our own little family Christmas dinner, and all but the spinach and mashed potatoes were from America! After we got Patty asleep we enjoyed arranging her things under the tree. We had a beautiful little rocker made in Abbottabad, and put a pretty new doll in it (S&H trading stamps!) We got three huge boxes from Hope Church, so both kiddies had lots of toys. Our national staff came at midnight and caroled until 1 a.m.!

Christmas morning we had Urdu worship out in the sunshine in front of the ward, and then the annual big feast of rice pilao and curry for all the staff. Afterwards we drove up to Muzuffarabad in free Kashmir to visit the Cutherells. It is only 35-40 miles but takes 2½ hours through the mountains. They were glad for visitors, as they are sort of isolated. Patty was glad to renew acquaintance with Luke and Robin, her playmates of last summer in Murree.

4

More Letters Home - 1958

Feb. 20. I'm afraid Nathan is getting spoiled, as Safedie the ayah holds him a lot. She was quite surprised when I told her it didn't hurt to let him cry. She said they believed it made a baby "weak" to let it cry! Of course, he loves being held. He will be 6 months old next week! There is a crazy man around here who has been shouting "Allah, uuh!" with quite a rhythm, constantly. I mentioned him to Safedie yesterday, and she said, "Oh, he is a very righteous man, a special slave of God." This is what they think of any demented person. Some days ago I came home from clinic for lunch, in a hurry as we had lots of patients yet to see. Patty was sleepy and crying, Nathan was howling for his food. We had a potpie of sorts from leftovers, as we were about out of things. Someone drove up in a big car, and Russ came in to ask if the vice-consul of the American Embassy in Lahore could eat with us! We weren't exactly prepared for such distinguished visitors, but he was very nice and seemed to enjoy the food. He was on his way to meet a plane in Peshawar with Henry Cabot Lodge, enroute to Afghanistan, and decided to meet some of his Americans in this area.

March 2. We attended a wedding feast in a village about 4 miles from here of a relative of Samunder Khan, our building crew director. We were met at the road's edge by a "band" of two bagpipes and several drums, the bridegroom, and Baba Samunder Khan. We were escorted half a mile to the village, and taken to a mud courtyard where we were further entertained by more musicians and two women professional dancers with bells jingling on their ankles. No other women were in sight! (Dancers are a different class, enjoyed but not considered proper.) There were just men and hoards of children on the nearby rooftops and courtyard walls! Then we were taken to another courtyard and served the meal. It soon started to rain, so we had to move inside to a little dark room without windows. Patty had a great time. She is always adored, as she is so friendly. "Baba" is her special friend. She spends a lot of time with him here on the hospital compound as he goes about his work. He carries her around, and lets her ride his horse. She is quite possessive and calls him "My Baba!" When she sits on his lap, she likes to play with the pistol, which he always carries. I trust it is not loaded!! He is sort of a grandfather figure for her.

April 13. Last Sunday was Easter, and Russ preached his first full length Urdu sermon in the morning service. He did very well! Patty looked adorable in her new coat, hat, and purse. Nathan is so happy, gurgling and "talking." Right now he is on the living room floor tearing up a magazine. It makes such a lovely noise! His first lower tooth finally appeared today!

April 26. In February a young lady came to us with a huge tumor in her abdomen. She had been turned away from several government hospitals as hopeless, and had been divorced by her husband because she was sick and of no use to him. She willingly put her life into our hands, and we operated. We were able to remove (with 3 hours of effort!) a 45-pound tumor from her. With the tumor, she weighed 105 pounds! She was critical for several days, but God granted her complete recovery and she is now a happy, healthy young woman! In March a pale, swollen young woman with hookworm anemia was brought in on a bed, just about to die. Her blood count was lower than our hemoglobinometer could register! With great technical difficulty due to lack of proper equipment, we transfused her with a little less than a pint of blood, the first transfusion ever given in this area. Her sister gave blood. She rallied and began to improve. When she was strong enough, we were able to treat her hookworm disease. After about 6 weeks with us, she was able to go home a different woman, once again able to walk and take care of herself. We hope that the gospel she heard time after time while she was here will have an effect on her life.

April 27. Russ and I, and the Belches (new missionary doctor and nurse) had a rare privilege last Friday. We were invited to a tea in honor of the Prime Minister of Pakistan, Malik Feroze Khan Noon. It was given in Abbottabad in a garden at the Army Officers Club, with a military band to furnish music. We were invited because the Nowab of

Phyllis Irwin, M.D.

Amb (father-in-law of the princess) was giving the tea, and remembered us from my visits to do pre-natal checks on the princess. Then yesterday evening, the Nowab of Amb came to visit the hospital, quite unexpectedly, accompanied by 3 burly bodyguards armed with rifles and cartridge belts. I showed them through the hospital and ward, and had a nice chat. Now today I received an engraved invitation from the Health Minister of Pakistan to a breakfast tomorrow morning, in Mansehra, in honor of the Prime Minister! I may be the only woman there except for the wife of the Prime Minister, an English lady!

May 11. The breakfast with the Prime Minister was very interesting, held at the Government Rest House in Mansehra, and attended by many of the local "khans" or headmen. This kind of meeting is called a durbar. I met a lot of big wheels—the Food Minister, the Health Minister, and Lady Vicar-un-Nissa Noon, the PM's wife. There was quite a spread of food, including roast chicken. I was glad to get away from it, though, and back to my waiting patients.

Just a couple of hours ago we "adopted" a baby! A 3-pound baby was born to a paralyzed lady with huge bedsores a couple of weeks ago. The sores were covered in cow dung when she came! The baby seemed to do fairly well with a relative feeding it from a bottle. The mother did not improve, and died a week ago. The husband has become our hospital "sweeper" (latrine cleaner), and lives in staff quarters with his 3 other little girls and a relative who cares for them. I went down to see the baby tonight, and found it almost dead. Dehydrated, not feeding, and diarrhea. I asked if I could take it home with me for a few days to see if I could do anything for it, and they willingly "gave" it to me! Some day maybe we'll have a hospital nursery and staff for sick babies! Her name is Miracle, and it certainly will be one if she lives. I am trying to feed her with a dropper, and have hot water bottles in the basket. I doubt if she lives, but we'll try. When I look at Nathan after caring for her, he looks like a giant!

This is picturesque wheat harvest time. The folks in their small fields cut each stalk with a hand sickle, bind them together, and later the oxen walk over it to thresh out the grain. It is then winnowed by the men painstakingly throwing it in the air with pitchforks. Another picturesque occasion this time of year is the moving back up north to the Kaghan Valley of huge flocks of sheep and goats. The numerous families move with them, returning from the south to their summer mountain pastures. The road is blocked every couple of miles with huge flocks of animals, many with baby lambs and goats. Coming separately behind are the families, the women walking along with all their possessions on their heads, carrying little babies. A few donkeys carry more possessions and small children.

July 26. Even though we tried a feeding tube on Miracle, she died after a few days. Patty was quite nuts about her. We had a man die of typhoid (perforated intestine) and Russ had to haul the body home 35 miles to Haripur at 1:30 a.m.!

Sept. 14. Since Dr. K. is on furlough, Dr. Christy or Dr. Brown is coming once a month to do eye operations. We had about 20 for Dr. Christy last Thursday. It is nice to have the ward full again with the opportunity to preach to more. It is also wonderful to be able to tell the cataract patients they can have their operations instead of turning them away. I wish I could have gotten a picture last week as we were driving to the dispensary at Brarkot. An old man, blind, that I had seen the week before at Brarkot, was being led across a dry riverbed by his son, who had a heavy roll of bedclothes on his back. They were on their way to Bach for his operations. We stopped and assured them to go on, that everything was ready for them. How we pray their spiritual eyes will be opened while they are at the hospital.

Nov. 1. We visited Campbellpur for a few days of left over vacation. Davises have 9 new Alsatian puppies, and Nathan went wild over them. Patty and Marie went wading in the nearby river, while Bill and Russ went swimming. I was tempted, but it was not   private—about 100 soldiers came just as we left, to wash their clothes and bathe! Sunday afternoon there was a birthday party for Charlie Davis, 9 years old, with a cake decorated like an American flag!

Coming home, we visited all our mission stations on the way. Campbellpur is the southernmost. Then saw the Vern Rocks in their newly opened station in Hussan Abdul, Haripur with the Stoddards and Walter Montgomery, then Havelian where the DeHarts are. Patty and Timmy had a little tea party, and then we pushed on to Abbottabad and Bach.

Tonight all the missionary staff from the hospital was invited to the home of Sardar Bahadur Khan, brother of President of Pakistan,

Phyllis Irwin, M.D.

Ayub Khan. I have visited this home twice before in official capacity, for his mother, and then his wife. We missionary women ate with the men downstairs, a delicious Pakistani buffet. Patty always makes a big hit with her blonde hair and talkative ways. After eating, we women went upstairs to visit with the wife and daughter. They are in purdah (seclusion), so don't get to come downstairs when there are men who are not family members.

5

Stories From My Diary

*N*ov. 1959

Sometimes our small living quarter at Bach Hospital seemed to be the hub of activity. One evening before supper we had a three-ring circus going in the only heated area, the living room. After a day seeing patients in the clinic, I was bathing Patty and Nate, ages four and two, in a corner in an oblong galvanized laundry tub. We were close to the small wood drum stove to keep warm.

While doing this, I was talking to Betty Burton about the practical use of medicines. She was a nurse and was learning to be a primary screener to see clinic patients. In another corner, Safedie, our ayah (nanny), was giving baby Nikki a bottle. We had acquired this baby four days before from a family just across the road from the hospital. The mother had died in childbirth from a retained placenta with hemorrhage. They had not brought the woman to the hospital when she was in trouble, but now they felt helpless to care for this tiny newborn girl, weighing only four pounds. On my offer, it was turned over to us for a few weeks. We had no nursery at the hospital at that time, and no staff to care for it, so she was with us. The kids were delighted to have a baby in our home and loved to hold and help feed her. We planned to teach the grandmother how to properly bottle feed and care for her. Meanwhile, Safedie was helping out and learning, too.

In another corner at the table, missionary auditors Ed and Walt were working on hospital books with Russ. A knock at the door, and Lawyer Akram from Muzuffarabad (thirty miles away in Azad Kashmir) came in all bedraggled and wet. He had walked twelve miles in the rain, as the road on the side of the mountain had washed out again. He was a good friend and interested in the Scriptures. He had come to spend the night with us. In due time, we all had supper together which Sher had prepared. How thankful I was for his help, and for Safedie's! Later Russ showed slides and I served refreshments.

CLINIC STORIES AND HEPATITIS

THERE WERE ONLY 80 patients for me to see in clinic Friday. I enjoyed taking more time with them, and chatting with a few. One, a 12-year old girl, told me she had been married for a year. Complaint? She had not become pregnant yet! Another lady told me her husband had married a second wife, because she had produced only a baby daughter for him. So he married wife #2, but later thought she had been unfaithful, so he cut off her nose (a usual punishment for suspected unfaithfulness.) Then he proceeded to marry her sister for a third wife! Oh, the depth of the sorrow and mistreatment of these women.

On May 12, Andrew and Olive Karsgaard left for India to be with their children at Musoorie at the missionary children's school. I was the lone doctor at the hospital. Days went something like this: "Rounds on 70 in-patients, and 149 outpatients in clinic." Another day, "I must have malaria, as I have fever." Next day I felt like the morning after! Dizzy and weak, I managed to get up to the hospital. Limited patient numbers to 75 but ended up seeing 101. I had to rest a couple of times in the other exam room. Another day rounds took over two hours, and we discharged many eye surgery patients. After three minor surgeries, an emergency came in. A man had fallen down a ravine while cutting grass for his cattle. We did what we could for his injuries, but he died of massive head injury within two hours. I was called back to the hospital for a bleeding lady with an incomplete abortion. I did a D&C and went back to my kids. They are good about Mommy being gone so much.

By the end of May, still the lone doctor, I was still seeing 130 or so daily in the clinic. On the 28th, I felt dizzy and fatigued, with a low-grade fever. Russ bathed the kids, and I stayed in bed all afternoon. The next day was Sunday, and I was so weak and dizzy I couldn't make rounds. I had a fever, but decided this probably was not malaria. So what was it? On Monday I felt some better, and Russ helped me walk up to the hospital. I slowly made rounds by sitting on each bed. I was so weak I couldn't stand very long. Norma Culler helped me see the clinic, and then I went back to bed. Tuesday I felt better again in the early morning, but soon I vomited. I literally dragged through rounds, and had to lie down on the exam table in the other clinic room every few patients. Finally I looked at myself in a small mirror. My eyes were very yellow!! The lab confirmed the diagnosis of hepatitis. With that diagnosis, I realized I could not carry on. Norma finished clinic and Russ helped put a cast on a patient!! It was sooo good to go to bed and have an excuse for it. Now I would have weeks in bed. We had to call our new doctor in language study to come down from Murree until Dr. Karsgaard could get back from India.

I felt apologetic as Dr. Karsgaard, his vacation cut short, came into my bedroom a few days later. "Well, I see you have the missionary measles!" was his comment. I became very yellow all over, and then came the incessant, unrelievable itching. Weakness was marked. If I just got up to straighten my sheet a bit, I was exhausted. Safedie was so good, taking care of the kids, scratching my back, and being sympathetic. I had lots of visitors, as according to the culture, friends and acquaintances were bound to come! We finally had to post "visiting hours" on our outside door so I could get some rest! Russ was a constant nurse and companion. I was able to sit up and share with him an eighth wedding anniversary dinner in the bedroom. There were bright spots of humor, too. One day Nathan (age three) was standing on the steamer trunk in our bedroom pretending to be a preacher, as he had often observed his daddy. He pointed his finger at his imaginary audience and admonished, "Never, never write on the walls with crayons!"

By mid June it was daily over 100 degrees outside and 90 in the bedroom. There was no outside window, and no air conditioning. By the end of June, I was able to study Urdu for a couple of hours a day with Mr. Durrani. I was working on Pilgrim's Progress for the third year Urdu test, the only part remaining. Marianne and Ginny Brown were good to help with the children when Russ had to be gone and Safedie was off duty.

In mid July I was able to make a liver-jarring jeep trip with the family to the Kaghan valley for a camping trip. We were three families, complete with cooks and all our supplies. This proved to be a time of real recovery, in the cool mountain air, camping in a tent by the rushing Kunhar River. The men enjoyed hiking up the nearby glaciers. I was content with short walks by the river. The children enjoyed splashing in a shallow backwater of the river, and it was an adventure for the mommies to wash clothes in the stream! Patients began to visit our camp when they learned of the doctor's presence, and we began to visit some of their homes. My strength returned, and by August 1, I was able to resume my duties at the hospital on a part time basis.

6

The Princess Of Amb

*P*atty, as a toddler of about 18 months, played with a real princess in 1957 as we made a trip to Amb. The state of Amb is about 290 square miles, a tiny patch on the banks of the Indus in northern Pakistan. At the time of our arrival in Pakistan, it was still a semi-independent state, with its own ruler, the Nowab. Amb was still under a feudal system, with all the land owned by the Nawab, and his people the sharecroppers. He had his own law enforcement, and his word was the final authority in any matter. He was quite wealthy and was impressed with his own importance although he was just a little slip of a man. He had an only son, the prince, who was married to a lady from the royal family of Chitral, a larger state to the west.

The princess was about to have their first baby, which would be important in direct line of succession. I was asked to officiate at the big event, and of course, I must produce a boy if at all possible! Bach Christian Hospital's new lady doctor had come to the Nawab's attention through his lawyer, who lived in Abbottabad a few miles from our hospital. Lawyer Jan was a good friend of Dr. Karsgaard who had started the medical work.

Patty, Mrs.Shah my clinic translator, and I made the first 22 miles of the journey with Lawyer Jan in his car. The last 27 miles was made in the Nawab's jeep, because of the terrifically rough, rocky road. Unpaved, it wound along cliffs overlooking the mighty Indus. This was quite an adventure for me, as I was still in language study trying to make sense of the difficult Urdu, and had not ventured out much.

We arrived at Darband, the capitol city of about 10,000, one late Saturday afternoon. Right on the banks of the river, Darband looks like any other big village, except for the Nawab's grounds and gardens.

We stayed in the guest house, reserved for us and the lawyer. There was no electricity, but the house was furnished elegantly with thick Persian carpets. One of the Nawab's secretaries (I called him Secretary of State) was designated to be our host, as he spoke good English. We were served delicious roast partridge, hunted by the Nowab himself with his hooded falcons just like in medieval times! We were shown around the gardens and orange groves, and picked the tasty oranges known as "blood oranges" for their red flesh.

On Sunday morning, I took Patty with me to the harem (that's the word they used!) to see the women. They lived in strict seclusion, and guards kept any man from even getting near them, except for the Nowab and Prince! When we entered the courtyard surrounded by mud walls, the women immediately were fascinated by Patty! I guess they had never seen a white baby before--and she was sort of fetching!! The Princess took her at once; Patty "salaamed" her and made friends! We went into the Princess's room for the pre-natal examination. The quarters were not much different than most of the mud houses, except for the expensive furniture, rugs, drapes, and a radio. They heated with an open fireplace.

The Princess was lovely—quite fair, with naturally curly dark hair and an Oriental look to her eyes. My examination indicated that she had some symptoms of pre-eclampsia (toxemia), and I advised that she come to the hospital for delivery.

The next day before we left, we had an audience with the Nowab. A guard with a big rifle guarded the door to his courtyard, and several more bodyguards with cartridge belts over their shoulders surrounded the Nowab in his audience room. The Nowab is a small, bespectacled man who speaks no English. He preferred that we, with all the nurses and other personnel and equipment necessary, move en masse to Darband

Phyllis Irwin, M.D.

to stay until after the delivery! I thought we persuaded him otherwise, but I had much to learn!

Shortly after that first trip, the Lawyer Jan came to me and said the Nowab would not allow the princess to come to the hospital for the delivery, and wanted me to go there to Amb State. I arranged to go, to examine her again and perhaps persuade him to allow her to come. One of our lady teachers from the Missionary Children's School in Abbottabad, Mary Erb, was going with me to translate.

A car was to pick us up at 9 a.m.. It arrived at 1:30 p.m.. I refused to go, and told them to come back in the morning at 7:30 a.m.. The next day the car did show up at 9 a.m., so we started out. Hard rain had made the unpaved roads very difficult, but the driver said they were passable. We were in a Chevrolet "taxi" as all the Nawab's vehicles were tied up. It took us 5 hours to make the 3-hour trip. The taxi broke down twice, with the driver repairing it by the roadside.

We stopped first to see the Nawab, who was in a different village hunting partridges with his trained falcons. We again thought we persuaded him to allow the Princess to go to the hospital for delivery, if I would stay until they got things ready. How naive I was! We drove on to Darband. Mary went with me to the harem, where the women were thrilled that she understood Urdu! The Princess was feeling good, still a few days from delivery. We urged them to come to us for delivery, as her blood pressure was up and she had albumin in the urine. Mary had to leave again the same day, but I agreed to stay until the next day and accompany the Princess personally.

Even though I was "alone" the rest of the day, I had plenty to do. When the women of the town heard I was there, they came swarming to the guest house to have the lady doctor see them. I did see many, prescribing simple medicines. They quite wondered about me as I was so different. I wore no burka, or veil. I treated them kindly, unlike the staff in their own civil hospitals. It was a good chance for me to practice my limited Urdu. Next day, I was disappointed to find the Princess herself said she would not go but preferred to stay right there. I'm sure she had been instructed to give that answer, and I decided not to further buck the culture! The Nawab's big Packard that was to take me back to Abbottabad would not start—dead battery I was told. This necessitated staying over another night and returning in an ancient "taxi." The suspension was shot, so it really bounced over the rough road, taking an hour to do the first 10 miles.

The trip was not altogether in vain, as I got an insight into the people I did not have before. I brought back a few gifts. One grateful woman gave me a nice embroidered piece, and the princess gave me a beautiful hand made piece in bright colors that almost looks like tapestry. However, the best things I brought back were two small, sweet, fuzzy, white puppy dogs! These purebreds belonged to the Princess, and looked like miniature Samoyeds. Only one was for us; the other was for Lawyer Jan. Patty just went wild with joy when she saw them, laughing and running after them.

The end of this part of the story is that they never called for me again for this delivery case. We heard indirectly that the baby had been born, and that it was a girl. Maybe just as well I didn't deliver it!

A year and a half later, in the summer of 1958, I got a note from the Nawab to come to his summer home and examine his wife for some eye trouble. The next Sunday Russ drove me, Patty, baby Nate and one of our nurses, Ruth Arvidson, up a few miles beyond Oghi, a town on the border of tribal territory. We had not been to his summer residence before. We were royally entertained in a separate guest house, with a huge living room furnished with Persian rugs, couches and chairs. There was a big cloth fan extending the width of the room, suspended from the ceiling with a rope attached. A servant man would sit on the floor by the door to pull the rope, drawing the fan back and forth. There was no electricity. We were served a cool drink (with unboiled water, no doubt, so we all renewed our typhoid shots the next day!) We had a delicious feast in the large dining room. Then we rested in the bedrooms for an hour or so before the children and I were summoned to the women's quarters to see the patient.

The Nawab's wife had immature cataracts, which didn't make her very happy. I noticed at once that the princess was again to be a mommy, but didn't comment. Just as we were about to leave, she asked me to examine her. (This was the real reason I had been called, but they had to approach it indirectly after the first case fiasco.) She was due very soon, and wanted very much for me to deliver her. This one MUST be a boy! After examining her, I had to go see another patient, the wife of some other high official in the tiny kingdom. While I was busy with this house call, Russ had a talk with the Nawab. He seemed quite interested in religion, and asked Russ to bring someone with him next time who could fluently speak Urdu! He wants to talk and debate at length about Christianity.

Back at the hospital the next day I was fixing supper after a day at the clinic when a messenger came from the Princess saying she was in labor. He asked us to go right away. It had taken the man 7 hours to get to us, so I figured the baby would already have been born. We got ready and went anyway. Russ drove, and we took Patty and Mrs. Shah. It took us 2 hours to get there, going through several streams and rivers. Thankfully, the water was shallow.

When we arrived, we heard the drums beating in celebration and knew that a son had been born. He had arrived five hours earlier, with only her mother-in-law attending (the one with cataracts!). The Nawab had gone to Abbottabad to meet the Prime Minister, and left her without any car to send for help! The messenger had come by bus, which broke down, so he was delayed.

However, we were there to give the baby its first bath, examine the mother and comfort her. What a shame such an intelligent and beautiful lady has to be stuck away in seclusion without any outside contacts. Russ and Mrs. Shah left the next morning, but I stayed on with Patty. We spent most of the day in the women's courtyard, with the princess and baby. There were a lot of lady guests and well-wishers, and the drums never ceased beating all day. The women had quite a reaction to Patty's doll with moveable eyes. They thought it was simply the most wonderful thing they had ever seen and took turns holding it! It was more interesting than the new prince! Patty didn't seem to mind, and her friendliness really bonded us to those women. Late afternoon we were driven home in the Nawab's jeep, which had returned.

We learned from someone who knew the Nawab well that he was very upset over the plans by the central government to build the huge Mangla Dam across the Indus to generate electricity for a large part of the country. His anxiety was well founded, for then his capitol city Darband would be under water, and the citizens relocated to another area. He tried to dissuade the engineers who came to survey. "Please tell the president that it would be a big waste of money to build a dam here. I had my own seer examine the water, and there is no electricity in it!" (Ed.

Note: Some years later, after the Nawab had died, the great Mangla Dam was built, the people relocated, and the kingdom is gone.)

Two years had elapsed when a jeep came with a man from the Nawab of Amb asking me to once again go and examine the princess, now expecting her third. This time Patty and Nathan both went with me. We left Daddy at home. After a rough jeep ride in the dark, we got to the summer residence of Shergard late at night. After sleeping in the guest house, the children woke early and began exploring. "Bed tea" was brought at 6 a.m.; breakfast at 8. I had Sunday School with the kids while waiting. The princess was very lovely and seemed glad to see us. She is due in a week or two, so I arranged to return and wait for her delivery, as they had wanted me to several years before! I was not back to full time duty at the hospital following a debilitating bout with hepatitis a few weeks earlier, so I could arrange time off. I would miss my third year Urdu exam in September, but this event seemed the higher priority.

On September 2, 1960, Patty, Nate, I, Ginger Lundgren and Val (Patty's age) left in a taxi provided by the Nawab, to stay until the princess delivered. She seemed ready to go into labor any day. We visited the women daily and took presents to the princess's two children and for the expected baby. We were even allowed to take pictures (the Nawab didn't know and the women were willing!). Our three children played with the children there in the courtyard. I saw patients, gave out medicines and cholera shots. Darband at that time was quarantined because of cholera in the area. One afternoon we were in the outer courtyard with the women and children. When they heard the Nawab's jeep arrive, they quickly scurried back into the inner courtyard! Begum Sahiba, the wife of the ruler, said "Your life is good; our life is no life at all." One day when we were in an inner room with the women, one of them said, "Watch how we take a walk outside!" She then peeked through a small hole in the heavily curtained window to see a bit of the world outside their courtyard!

On the fifth night we had a rat in our bedroom! As long as I spot-lighted it with the flashlight, it would "freeze" but as soon as I turned the light off, it would scamper around again. I finally gave up, tucked the mosquito net firmly around Patty's bed, and tried to sleep. The next day we gave more cholera shots in the harem and went out to another home to see the three wives of the obese chief of police. No sign of a baby yet! I fed the Princess quinine and castor oil, and gave her an enema to try to induce labor. We held clinic every day in the rest house before going to the harem.

On September 7 we were returning from the harem in the evening, and were overjoyed to see Russ and Paul, our husbands, arriving in our VW van! Russ had been in Murree and had passed his fifth year Urdu exam! How I wished I had been able to take my third. That evening word came that the princess was in labor. Ginger and I stayed with her all night, but her contractions stopped at 2 a.m.. On the 10th September, Russ and Paul had to leave, taking the children. Ginger and I were there alone. That day the princess showed us her wedding clothes and jewelry, all packed away unused. There were many beautiful types of brocade and real silks, and much gold jewelry. That evening I had a good chance to witness to the Prince, Princess, and the Begum Sahiba. The Princess asked for my copy of Pilgrim's Progress in Urdu, which I was studying for my third year exam. I gladly gave it to her, thankful that she was interested!

On the eleventh, a prince is born! During the morning I had a big clinic on the Persian carpet of the guest house and didn't get to the harem until 11 a.m.. The Princess consented to rupturing membranes, which I promptly did. She started labor half an hour later, and progressed rapidly. Around 4 p.m. the baby arrived, with a mad dash for me at the last to get her draped and keep the midwife from getting her unwashed hands in the way! All went well, and we soon had a cute baby boy. The drums started beating to announce his arrival.

The next day I had a big clinic on the guest house porch, before Ginger and I were called to the Nawab's chamber for an audience. All his armed guards were surrounding him, and as usual, he wanted to argue religion. When he felt he had "put us in our place", we were allowed to go back to the harem. We visited with the Princess, bathed the new Prince and dressed him up for pictures. After a quick lunch at the guest house, and more patients, we had one last visit. The Princess gave both Ginger and me beautiful Benares silk pieces and several hand worked pieces. The women almost cried when we left in the jeep at 4 p.m.. But it was so good to get HOME to MY family!

Two months later Patty, Nate, Jean Sodemann (a nurse) and I went to Darband to circumcise the new little Prince. I also did a post partum check up on the Princess. The baby is fat and healthy, and she is happy to be the mother of two sons. I gave her some advice and a method of family planning, which the Nawab later somehow got word of. He was very upset, and never called for me again. I had to wait to do the circumcision until permission came from the Nawab and the Imam (religious leader.) They had to check with the astrologers first to see if the day was auspicious. While we waited, the children got to play on the sand banks of the Indus. After the event, the drums were started and the celebration begun. We drove home in our own vehicle later that day.

We will not know in this life what impact our visits, witness, and that copy of Pilgrim's Progress really had on the people we visited in Amb. Ten years later, we were in the high Himalayan state of Chitral, the full story of which is in another chapter. We were visiting the sister of the princess, who was the ruler of Chitral. The princess was dead, of kidney complications of repeated pregnancies for which I was not called. But at her death, the Mehtar (ruler) of Chitral had taken her copy of Pilgrim's Progress, which she proudly showed to us when we visited her palace.

7

Compassion

"*W*hen he saw the crowds, he had compassion on them, because they were harassed and helpless..." Compassion, when shown to helpless and hopeless patients at Bach Christian Hospital, goes a long way to show the compassion of Jesus, even when we cannot help. One day I was "screening charpais." Very sick bed patients are brought in, not by ambulance, but by being carried on wooden, rope strung beds called charpais. Each clinic day they are lined up outside the clinic, waiting for attention.

When I came to this woman, I was aghast to see, underneath the bed coverings, that she had third degree burns over most of her body. There were no burn dressings over her charred skin, but just a sheet. Her eyes pleaded with me for relief, though she couldn't speak. The relatives gave a story of some accident from the open wood fire that is used for cooking. I knew that the true story was more likely one of deliberate burning for some offense supposedly committed, or else a suicide attempt by the desperate woman herself. With no other means of ending her miserable life, fire was the only option. What untold tragedy was behind this?

I realized that we had absolutely no capacity to admit her for care. We already had several burn patients on the ward, and the overworked nursing staff could barely cope with the inordinate amount of care that such patients need. To admit one more would be the "straw that broke the camel's back." As I turned to explain to the relatives the situation, there were unbidden tears in my eyes, and I just about broke down. It was the first and only time we had to turn away such a patient. I could only advise that they take her to the government hospital, where I knew she would NOT be adequately cared for. We were the only "burn center" in the whole Northwest Frontier Province, unsophisticated though our

Phyllis Irwin, M.D.

care might be. To my surprise and relief, the man I was speaking with did not object, cajole and beg as I had expected, but seemed to actually be concerned for me! He did not anticipate that the doctor would be so touched. Sometimes it is unexpectedly helpful to show emotion when dealing with a patient, although usually the doctor must remain rather detached from such demonstrations. They quietly took her away to die. How I wished I could have been able, like Jesus, to say, "Woman, be healed!" But I am not Jesus, although I want to be more like him in compassion and character.

Rehmat Jan would show up at the hospital every year or two, when she was in a leprosy reaction following the birth of a child. Leprosy is a strange and complicated disease, requiring long term care and medication. With a reaction, the entire body surface can break out into enormous, sloughing, weeping sores. This happened to Rehmat Jan every time she would have a baby. Her husband would fail to bring her regularly for medication, in spite of instructions. Only when she was covered with filthy sores and repulsive to be around would he go to the trouble to bring her to the hospital. What a pathetic picture this poor woman would make, clutching her beautiful newborn baby with its flawless skin next to her diseased flesh.

Our young Pakistani nurse aides, who were Christian girls trained in our own hospital, would take the babe to bathe and dress, putting it in a separate cot while they worked on the mother. Then they would lovingly take that untouchable, filthy mother and clean her up so gently, bandage her wounds, wrap her in a soft gown, and put her in a clean bed.

This would go on for days as she slowly healed and responded to medication. Compassionate love shown by touching the untouchable, loving the unlovable, dressing the dreadful, was a more powerful expression of the Gospel than any spoken word. She heard the Word, too, as Scripture was simply explained in the ward daily. I wish I could say that she became a believer in Jesus, but there was no outward evidence of that. Finally healed and grateful, she would be taken home with a supply of medicine. We would exhort the husband to come back for her medication, but feared we would not see her again until she was once more in that unspeakable state.

Sakari was brought in on a rope bed from high up in the Kohistan mountains. Patients from that far away are usually in desperate straits by the time they reach Bach Christian Hospital. She certainly was, having fallen down a slope suffering a compound (open) fracture of her right leg. Days old, with the bone ends visible and oozing with infection, the fracture was untreatable.

But this spunky little lady had survived a cruelly painful trip carried on a bed and jostled on a bus for a full 18 hours. In addition to her injury, on exam she was found also to have tuberculosis of the spine, with a khyphosis (humpback.) While her TB was being treated, the relatives were advised that the next step was to amputate the leg. For this surgery, she would need blood as she was very anemic. Impossible!! What good is a woman, or a man, for that matter, in the mountains with only one leg? And give blood? No, thanks!! (Our blood bank is a walking one consisting of the relatives, who often refuse to give.) No persuasion worked for either surgery or blood. The relatives all "disappeared" leaving her in the care of her 12-year old son. After a few days, an adult relative appeared and reluctantly gave permission to amputate. But no blood! They have to conserve their own for the frequent blood feuds up in the hills. The 12-year old son offered to give, but his blood type was not compatible.

However, my blood type was the same as Sakari's. One day I had a pint of blood drawn in the lab, and then took her to surgery for the amputation. While my blood was being infused into her, I cut off that stinking leg, glad to have the job done! The next morning on rounds, her formerly dark, sullen, depressed face was full of light and wreathed in smiles! We could not speak her mountain dialect, but her son had told her that the doctor had given her blood so she could have the operation. What a difference a demonstration of compassion had made! She hugged me, and thereafter made a good recovery. Every day on rounds she was bright and cheerful. After being fitted for wooden crutches, she went home to her mountains. She had not been able to understand the Gospel in words, but she responded to love and compassion.

Now, the rest of this story is that twenty five years later, shortly before retirement, I was able to find this woman on my first and only trek up into those awesome mountains. Word had reached her that we were looking for her. As we climbed toward her mud-stone house, she scampered down the slope to meet us. This once-doomed patient was bounding down the rocky trail like a mountain goat—on one leg and one stick! She had long ago changed the crutches for one stick with a padded crosspiece under her armpit. She was quite hale and hardy, and grateful for the health she had been given. We could only communicate with smiles and hugs, but compassion had made a difference. She welcomed us to her humble hut, and offered us walnuts and tea. What a joy to see this remarkable woman surviving so well in her harsh surroundings.

Two distraught men came hurriedly one morning into the ward while I was making rounds. "Something has happened to the Ghorda-wala Khan (headman who owns horses). Come quickly!" The men and I started at once in our VW van up the bumpy road to the nearby village. As we drove, I thought of the kindly man who for years had given our children rides on his big, handsome horses, who was always so robust, friendly and full of good humor. I thought of his wife, who had been a patient at one time when their 13th child was born.

As we neared the village, someone on the path told us that the khan had already died. While we were yet on the footpath to the house, the sounds of wailing and mourning could be heard, joining with the cries of the men who were with me. Solemn faced men were clustered outside the courtyard. In the middle of the courtyard was the rope bed on which the khan's body lay, surrounded by packed throngs of women and children weeping, wailing, and striking their faces and chests in the throes of grief. Another hundred or so mourners were crowding the rooftops around the courtyard.

When I came in, the crowd parted a little and quieted down while I bent over to examine him. When I shook my head to their anxious questions, "Is he still alive," the noise of mourning broke out with renewed force. My heart went out to my Muslim sisters in the hopelessness of their grief, and I wept with them. As I clasped the khan's wife to me, what words of comfort could I offer? All these hundreds of weeping people, with no hope because they do not know the Savior burdened my heart as never before. Oh, that they might know my Christ!

8

Trek To Tribal Area

OCTOBER 1966

When Sir Edmund Hilary and Tenzing Norgay conquered Mt. Everest in 1953, they never revealed which one actually stepped on the summit first. A pale comparison in our missionary experience was when Jenny Thompson and I stepped together over a small stream, which divided Tribal Territory from the government controlled area of The Northwest Frontier Province of Pakistan. We were told that we were the first white women ever to visit that area. We wanted it to be known that we had entered together!

The farthest outpost the British held during the English occupation in this province was Oghi, where the large fort is still used by Pakistani police. Beyond Oghi, where we had for years made monthly clinic trips, lies a large area of mountains and valleys stretching to the Indus, beyond which is Swat. Most of this area has become "merged", which means that it has come under the control of the government of Pakistan and has some degree of law and order. There are still large areas of Kohistan to the north, and areas to the south along the Indus, which at that time were still tribal areas. In those areas there has been nothing but tribal law, the law of the gun! No schools, no post offices, no medical facilities exist, and blood feuds are carried on for generations. Most of the men are armed with rifles and cartridge belts.

We have had patients from these areas for years, often gun shot wounds. One of these had been a young man who had been shot in the abdomen. Another was an old man who needed surgery from an old gunshot wound. The day after Dr. Bob Blanchard arrived in Pakistan he operated on the first boy, and missionaries donated blood. His life was saved. The next day Dr. Bob operated on the old man, the head of his village area. Again, his life was miraculously preserved and he was restored to health. While they were at the hospital, they heard the Gospel story in their own Pushto tongue, from Jack Ringer. The old man, Lal Saeed, said, "These things are in my heart; I will not forget." When he left we told him that some day we would visit him in tribal area, and he responded with a cordial invitation.

After months of planning and waiting, this trip became a reality. In October 1966, Jenny and Dick Thompson, Russ, Cindy (who was five at the time) and I set out in our VW van, taking with us a patient and his relative as far as Oghi. This man had been admitted two months before, with a fulminating infection in his right leg and foot due to some "home treatment" of a minor wound. It seemed initially that the leg would have to be amputated, but he got by with only two toes amputated. After skin grafting, he finally healed.

Leaving Oghi, we drove over rough switchback unpaved roads to Quza Banda. We stayed the night in a government rest house. Quvat Khan, an old friend and the headman of that village, was expecting us and brought our evening meal. This was spread on a cloth on the floor of the bedroom. His compound was very near, and the next morning early we set out across the fields and through a stream to his house for breakfast. This was served in his guest room, a mud hut with thatched roof. The menu was tea, chicken, and paratas. Paratas are a type of delicious flat bread saturated with clarified butter and baked over an open fire. Then Jenny, Cindy, and I were taken back to the women's quarters to see his wife, mother, daughters, and assorted female relatives. After proper greetings, I was busy seeing patients. The mother was an old TB patient of mine, and several children were brought with worms, fevers, and anemias. While I was occupied, Jenny watched one of the women at the open fireplace in the courtyard prepare the area's famous flattened roasted chicken, all pressed out in one big piece. Cindy, meanwhile, was quite the attention getter with her flaxen hair and outgoing, friendly personality.

When we returned to the rest house, we dispensed medicines from the van for the patients we had just seen. Several more sick ones appeared on the spot. Men from Yusaf Khan's village were urging us to finish and go with them to that village where we were invited for lunch. This involved a long trek through rice paddies, where the harvest had recently been cut, then down and across a small river by jumping from rock to rock, then up and up a hillside to the village. The Khan's house commanded an inspiring view of the valley and surrounding ranges. Each village has a watch tower from which to spot any approaching enemy.

We had a magnificent feast with many curries and vegetables. Then it was time for Jenny and me to visit the women's courtyard. This is the only time we ever see the women. They are never in evidence in the guest rooms where the Khans entertain. Men servants wait on the table (which is a cloth on the floor!) As we walked to the women's quarters we passed the miserable huts of the servants, with animals, filth, and babies all together in abundance. The Khan apologized, "These are poor people." I thought - but could not say - "And who is responsible for them more than you, with your rich house, food and clothes?" Inside, we met his two wives. The new one was bashful; the first wife was nicely clothed but obviously rejected—perhaps because she had given him only two daughters and no sons. Our clinic got so busy that Jenny, even though she is non-medical, started taking pulses just to give the women attention! We had a cup of tea, and rejoined the men and Cindy to start down the hillside. We made a stop at another small hamlet—another Khan—more tea with eggs and partridge—another clinic in the women's quarters. By now it was dusk, and we begged to leave.

We hastened back to Quza Banda, but had one more official stop before returning to the rest house. We visited the brother of Quvat Kahn, who somehow was on the outs with him, so we had to make a separate visit. Yes—more tea and eggs, and a visit to his women! I had done a C. Section on one of his wives, and found that she had carefully kept on the bandage for weeks, even though it was now tattered and dirty. I removed it and reassured her that the wound was well healed! By now we were so full of food we begged to be excused from an evening meal!

We went back to the rest house and started dispensing medicine for the many patients we had seen during the day. One or two men came back with us from each place to get the medicines, which we carefully labeled for each patient. One lady was brought in after dark, heavily veiled in her burka. She came to get an injection we had prescribed in one of the villages. One man brought a baby for amputation of an extra finger on each hand, attached only by a tiny bit of flesh. We soaked Russ's razor blade in antiseptic; Jenny held the baby, and I "operated." Surgery successful! It was quite late when we got all the medical work finished and could retire.

In the morning, we were off to Takot on the Indus, despite entreaties by our host Quvat Khan not to go. When he learned we planned to go into tribal area, he and his men tried to discourage us in every way. "The road is terrible, you can't make it. You may be killed. If something happens to you, we will be held responsible." These were a few of the arguments. However, we had perfect peace about it as we felt God definitely leading.

We started on what we had been told was a "one hour drive" by the men of Lal Saeed, our ultimate host. Soon it was evident that the journey was not to be so swift, although it was only about twenty miles. Just after starting, we went through a rough stream, but the VW slithered through some deep muddy spots without getting stuck. The weather was sunny and the scenery gorgeous. We marveled at the tiny terraced fields on the mountainsides, the mud houses perched tenuously in impossible places. I could understand why women in childbirth difficulties were in such bad shape by the time they made it to Bach Hospital. For every one who did make it, there must be many who do not ever get the chance to be carried on a rope bed down to the hospital.

We passed the Batagram turnoff and neared the village Peshawarda. We made a necessary "rest stop" using the nearest bushes before we approached the village. Immediately, a patient materialized from nowhere, showing us his clinic card from Bach Hospital! He was a TB patient, so we dug out the necessary medicines for him. An old lady from a nearby mud house asked us to "rest a while and have some tea." However, we pushed on. In the village we saw the patient we had left in Oghi the day we started on trek, sitting in front of a tea shop. He had not been able to find a jeep to take him all the way to Takot. Our van could not take his extra load on that road. Soon a sizeable crowd gathered. Some were curious, some wanted medicine. A road workman told us flatly we could not go any farther. He said they were blasting on the road ahead and it was closed.

Knowing better than to accept anyone's word as final, we pushed on to see for ourselves. A couple of miles on, sure enough, there was a road crew working. The road was blocked by loose gravel, dirt and boulders in two places. Dick and Russ had a talk with the crew foreman, who agreed to have it cleared off for us to pass. He assured us that if we got through that, we would have it made! We decided to let Russ pilot the vehicle through, and we would walk. That way, if the van and Russ slid down several hundred feet to the valley, at least the rest of us would be on top of the situation! Russ inched the VW van through with just barely enough room, cliffs straight up on one side and straight down on the other! We set out again, thankful that God was watching over us. Then we came to a steep hill and curve which led across a stream. The VW couldn't do it with a load, so again the "excess baggage" got out and walked. Jenny and I found a dirty-faced kid with a severe eye infection, and gave him some eye ointment. The mother ran up to pronounce blessings on us! The VW bounced through the rocky stream, only to be stopped on the far side by an army barrier.

The boy on duty told us we could go no farther. Only army jeeps and jeeps with special permission could proceed. We showed him a letter from the Khan of Takot with our invitation, which could pass as "permission", but he declared that our vehicle could not make it. He said only jeeps had passed that way before. With just a little more talking, he opened the barrier! The mountains now seemed higher and the gorge deeper, but the narrow little ribbon of a road etched into the side of the cliff seemed - secure! For we were in God's keeping! A couple of miles on we met another road crew, supervised by an army officer. He looked quite stern, and we thought he would not allow us to pass. Dick and Russ climbed out to talk to him, and soon he broke into a big smile - he was lonesome! He could not speak Pushto, so could not talk to the workmen except through a translator. He was glad to talk to someone in Urdu! He had the men clear the road, and soon we were on our way once more. It seemed like Pilgrim's Progress! From there on we had no trouble, and we arrived at Takot at 10:30 a.m., only three and a half hours instead of one!

It was a thrill to approach the village and see the broad expanse of the smooth flowing Indus, with the tribal area of Swat on the far side. The small settlement of Takot was the residence of the Khan of the area, Jan Mohd Khan. He was a friend of Dick's and of the hospital. At that time there was no bridge across the Indus, and crossing was made by floating on rafts made of inflated sheep and goat skins. (Later, a bridge was built, and Dick was expelled from Pakistan on the charges that he was "spying" during the bridge building while he was on trek in that area.)

Cindy immediately got out onto the white sands of the Indus River bank, and took off her shoes. Jenny and I sat under a tree and tried our Pushto on some curious women who gathered. The men went to the Khan's house to announce our arrival. The women vanished when our men reappeared—just when we were getting somewhere in Pushto.

Although the Khan of Takot was not present, his young son insisted we have lunch before we started on the hiking leg of our journey into tribal area. (Takot is in merged area.) Hospitality is not to be spurned in this area, so in spite of the urgency to go on at once, we sat in an outer courtyard patiently while the women cooked the food. After rice pilao, chicken curry and tea, we could take our leave, leaving our van there in the care of the Khan's men. We were escorted by an armed guard sent by the Khan's son. The son of our host-to-be Lal Saeed, also accompanied us. This son had met us a couple of miles from Takot earlier, having walked the road to meet us.

The first thing we had to do was to wade across a tributary of the Indus. Our adventurous five year old preschooler was carried on the shoulders of Azad Khan, the watchman from our clinic in Oghi who had come with us. We waded water waist deep in our clothes, emerging with our shalwars (full cotton trousers) dripping wet. They soon dried in the bright sun. We followed a path along the Indus, up and down, along narrow cliff trails, then down and over white sands of the river bank, then up again. We passed through several small villages on the way, and every-where we were greeted by people waving their Bach Christian Hospital registration cards. They wanted to tell us their medical problems and be examined by the "doctor memsahiba." A quick diagnosis on the trail would ensue, with a "prescription" jotted on a scrap of paper and given to them. On our return, we would dispense the medicines from our van in the Khan's courtyard. When we came to the dividing line between the Khan of Takot's territory, and that of the Khan Lal Saeed, we had a change of guard. Our six armed guards were exchanged for six of Lal Saeed's, all equally armed.

As Jenny and I stepped over the narrow stream dividing the areas, it was the first time white western women had ever been in that area! The first mountain we could see, we were told, was the mountain on top of which lived the young man who had been operated on for the gunshot wound. We would love to have seen him, but it was too far away. He called me "Mother" after I gave blood for his surgery. I marveled at the faith they must have had in the mission hospital to have come such a distance with a critical patient. A bit farther a mud house was pointed out to be that of the patient whom we had brought as far as Oghi. He had not yet arrived home. We could not imagine how they had carried this 200 pound man over those rough trails on a rope bed. We had trouble navigating ourselves over the trail! They had carried him for 14 miles before they could get a jeep.

A man plowing in a field was pointed out as one of my old patients. I examined on the trail a woman who had TB of the elbow. When we came to a small village, we were besieged by patients! One old man in the mosque had been to the hospital for heart trouble, and wanted more medicine; others brought sick and malnourished babies for me to see. It must have been like this when the Lord Jesus walked from place to place. Oh, that we could show them the love he had for the masses.

Ahead on the trail, we were approached by a cluster of men, all with rifles and cartridge belts. Luckily, they were friendly! In fact, they had been sent by Lal Saeed to escort us into his village.

Phyllis Irwin, M.D.

At 5:30 p.m. we entered the walled village. I didn't see what was coming, so was not alarmed. But Russ thought for sure he was going to lose his wife by a trampling. Just as I was about to enter the gate, a huge water buffalo thundered by me with a near miss and beat me through the gate! Had I been in the entrance, I would have been crushed!

We were seated on rope beds under the trees, and Lal Saeed came to greet us. We were pleased to note how well he looked after his surgery at the hospital. Forty or fifty villagers crowded around to stare. A baby was brought and laid in my arms as he was breathing his last, near death from pneumonia. After examining him, I had to tell them that he would die soon. Rather than being disappointed that I could do nothing for him, they lauded me for accurately predicting his demise. One spokesman chided us for not being able to spend more time with them, as we told them we had to leave again in the morning. They wanted us for at least one whole day. I reminded him that he himself at the hospital had assured me it only took an hour to drive from Quza Banda, and that the trail was level for walking and the hike was not more than an hour or two. If that had been true, we would have arrived in the morning instead of dusk! He answered by saying that he knew if he had told me the truth, we would never have come!

Tea was brought, and the men massaged Dick and Russ to relieve the tiredness of the trail. We had not seen any women yet, so we ladies didn't get that service! When it got dark, a lantern was hung in the tree while the conversation went on. Later we were ushered into the room of a mud house, where a delicious feast was laid out on the floor. We sat on blankets and pillows while devouring the food. The host seldom eats with the guests. We were served alone while others stood around and watched us eat!

While still sitting on blankets on the floor, the clinic began! It was all very orderly. They brought patients in one by one and seated them in a chair, while I sat on the floor at their feet to examine them! The room was illuminated by flickering torch light, with the armed guardsmen still at attention with their rifles around the sides of the room. Many of the patients were women. The clinic went on and on, until I was ready to drop—except I was already on the floor! At 11 p.m. the line was finished, and everyone cleared out of the room. Rope beds were brought in, and we lay down as we were in our clothes, exhausted. Cindy had long since fallen asleep on the floor.

We were awakened early in the morning. After a trip to the corn-field, one of the men poured warm water out of a lota (type of pitcher) while we washed. Tea and paratas were brought for breakfast. Jenny and I then went to the women's quarters. She was as busy as I, feeling pulses, talking, reassuring. Many were the ones we had seen the night before, but wanted the attention all over again! We made a visit to Lal Saeed's courtyard to meet his wife--a real matriarch! As soon as proper, we begged our leave, and set out again on the rugged four hour trail. The sun was already high.

We were accompanied by 20 or so villagers and bodyguards, some of whom dropped out at various points along the way. Just as we left, Lal Saeed offered me 100 rupees. I was a bit embarrassed and didn't know what to do. Adroitly, Dick gave me a hint in English, so after politely thanking him for it, I gave it back to him. This seems to have been the proper thing to do, and all were happy. They also sent a gift goat along with us. We did not know it was a gift to us until we were well on the way. We protested politely, thanked them profusely, then the goat was also happily sent back to the village. Tribal protocol!

The trail did not seem any shorter than the day before. Cindy was quite glad to be carried by Daddy or one of the bodyguards a good part of the way. Where the trail went through a narrow passage between some huge rocks, a spot was pointed out to us as the place where two men had been shot to death recently by enemies hiding behind nearby rocks. We were thankful they told us this story as we were leaving instead of com-ing! We were glad to see the tributary river come into view, and waded in for the crossing.

While Russ and Dick fetched the car, Jenny, Cindy and I managed to wash up a bit down by the Indus, and change into dry clothes in an abandoned building. We had a busy time dispensing medicines from the van for all we had seen in the village and along the way. I wonder if the representatives for various patients really got the right medicines to the right patients with the right instructions! We were prevailed upon to go see a woman in a house nearby who was very ill. It turned out she was dying of a severe stroke. Again there was nothing we could do but pray with the family. One last cup of tea with the Khan of Takot, Jan Mohd Khan, had to be shared before we could leave.

The afternoon was wearing on as we set out in the VW for the return trip, past all the now-familiar hard spots and stream crossings. We stopped at Quza Banda only long enough to send a message to Quvat Khan that we had returned safely, and then drove on to the hospital in the dark. Arriving about 9 p.m., we praised God for the opportunities we had had, and for his wonderful watch care over us. My heart is burdened as never before for that vast area. The physical needs are astounding--thousands of people without one single doctor! The spiritual needs are even greater—thousands bound in the web of Islam, which provides no assurance of getting to heaven. Medicine is clearly the open door. May we be able to take advantage of it to reach these benighted ones for Christ!

9

Out Clinics

BRARKOT

Over the years, Bach Christian Hospital has operated several out clinics which the doctors visited regularly. These were in rather far flung places into the mountains. The first one of these was at Brarkot, a little village just a few yards over the border into Free Kashmir, the narrow strip that India was not "occupying." We had a missionary family, and later, two single nurses, stationed there full time. They saw some patients daily and helped organize the clinic on "doctor day." It was my duty to see this clinic on Wednesdays when I first started medical work after language study. It was about 30 miles from the hospital where we lived. After climbing to the pass on a narrow, winding road, we would descend to a riverbed, which was usually dry. There was no road and no bridge across, but traffic would make a path through the gravel of the riverbed. There were several smaller riverbeds to cross before arriving at the small, two-room building which was built of mud and thatch. I usually took Patty (pre-school) and at times Nate, along with Safedie our ayah (nanny) to take care of them. We had some real adventures on some of our trips. Here are a few:

One clinic day in March of 1959, I saw 90 patients, including two lepers, two far advanced TB patients never treated before, and a midget 3'10" who had a large hole in her bladder from childbirth injuries. In April I saw 144 patients in seven hours, including two by the wayside when a man flagged our VW van down. In June a psychotic man threw rocks at our VW, breaking the windshield and the side ventilator window. The patients were terrorized, and all tried to squeeze inside the small clinic. The police had to come and take him away. In July, we got across the big flooded dry wash only by George McMillan, our lab tech, wading in front to check for holes. I had been stuck once before by a back wheel hitting a hole, which flooded the rear engine with water. That time we had to abandon the vehicle in the river, and wade out to the side. Patty was just a wee tot then, but was a good soldier and did not cry as she saw the water swirling in the van door. This time, with George's guidance, we did make it through, but not through the next riverbed. We had to leave the VW in a village and go by Army jeep to the clinic. We only had 40 patients that day, due to the monsoons.

In August of 1959, at one clinic there was a 2½ year old patient who weighed ten pounds. I had never seen such a malnourished child. One patient, when asked to step on the scale by the nurse, put her head on it instead! She explained, "It is my head that hurts!" After one clinic I brought back a strangulated hernia patient who needed surgery. Others came by bus and were referred to the hospital if they needed more help than we could offer there.

One clinic day it rained and the roof leaked so badly it was hard to find a dry spot to write on the charts! We made it that time through the flooded riverbeds. But the next time we got stuck twice in mudslides, from which we extricated the VW by throwing rocks and branches under the wheels. However, at the next riverbed, we had to leave the VW and take a horse drawn tonga to the clinic. We were quite late, and the 60 waiting patients were restless, waiting in the rain. On return, it seemed the VW would not make it through the widest dry bed, as it was flooded even more. Russ was gone on a trip, and I wondered if I would get home to Patty and Nathan, who were in the care of one of our missionary nurses. A taxi driver assured me I could make it across farther downstream, and he waded in front of us, throwing rocks out of the way as we drove against the current to a place that was shallower.

We got home at 7:30 p.m., very thankful to be safe. The NEXT clinic, Russ drove as the roads were still bad. Again, we had to leave the VW at the last riverbed, and walk to the clinic. The time after that, I hired a beat up taxi, with two other staff members to make the journey.

In January of 1960 Kashmir became a hot political issue between Pakistan and India, and the government made us close the clinic. No missionaries or foreigners could live there, and we had to pull our missionaries from three places in Free Kashmir.

OGHI

OUR LONGEST RUNNING clinic was established at Oghi in the early 1960's. Oghi is northwest of the hospital over a mountain pass just on the edge of Tribal Territory, where the central government had not yet established rule. The last outlying fort of the British Army was located in Oghi, and is still used as a police post. A missionary couple, Jack and Elma Ringer, would spend two weeks a month at Oghi, in a very humble mud dwelling, and the doctor visit would occur during that time. Elma, a nurse from New Zealand, would see some patients daily, and refer some to return for the doctor to see. Jack, a British army veteran who had spent years in British India, was fluent in Pushto, the main language of the area. He had a jolly way of presenting the Gospel as he talked with patients. The facilities were primitive. The mud room where we saw patients had no running water, and one small light bulb when there was electricity. Available light was from a high transom and the open door to the verandah, which was usually crowded with waiting patients. On nice days, we would set up in the courtyard. Not very private, but a lot lighter!

Phyllis Irwin, M.D.

As we saw increasing numbers of patients, a nurse screener would see patients in the other room. Our record number in May of 1978 was 293 patients! We finally restricted patients to only women and children, but even then in May of 1979 Wendy and I saw 265.

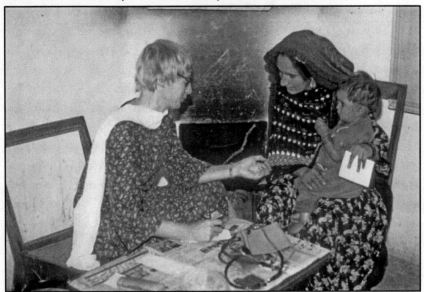

One day a young boy about 12 years came to be examined. He had been involved in the frequent feuds between rival clans, and had lost an eye to a gunshot wound. Nothing could be done but to advise him not to fight again! He told me that was not possible; he would certainly fight again, especially since the quarrel was not settled! With no police or law enforcement at that time in Tribal Territory, those tribal men were free to go at it anytime they wished. Clashes were usually over land disputes, or women, or money. In fact, there is a Pushto "proverb" we learned that feuds are always over Zamin (land), Zenana (women) or Zerd (yellow, meaning gold).

Cindy would often accompany me when she was a pre-schooler. At times a Pakistani staff child would also go so she would have a playmate. The clinic watchman, Azad Khan, would occasionally take them up to the watchtower on a hill, where the soldiers of the Raj used to spot enemy approaches. The trip in our VW van would take about an hour, if the roads were passable. Creeping up the switchbacks in first gear to the Susal Gali pass could be torture if we got behind a grinding, overloaded truck for there was no way to pass. We would have to close the windows to keep out the black, noxious diesel fumes from the exhaust. Once on the Agror plain, we had a river to cross just before the village of Oghi. This was usually a dry bed, but could flood during the monsoons. Cindy was with me once when we got stuck. Fortunately, a jeep came along at that time whose driver was kind enough to pull us out.

There were compensations for the poor roads, for we would enjoy magnificent views of gorgeous snow peaks in the distance, while watching close at hand the patient harvesters hand cutting wheat, binding it into sheaves. In other fields men and women were transplanting rice seedlings from their emerald green seed beds into the mucky fields. On days when we would finish clinic in good time, we would go across the field to the big house of the Khan of Agror, who owned the whole valley, and have tea with the ladies. Her husband was an educated agriculturalist and treated his tenants with respect. He was often out in the fields working with his men, which set him apart from other landlords in the area. His wife had an M.A. degree in art.

Their education was lacking in one area, however. The subject arose about which parent determines the sex of a child. During one of their trips to our hospital we invited them to our house for a cup of tea, which turned into a consultation about family planning.

The Khan spoke authoritatively, "The father deterrmines everything about the child, including the sex. You see, when I put a seed of corn in the ground, only corn will come up. The ground does nothing to determine whether wheat, corn, or rice comes up. The ground just provides nourishment for the seed." I felt the need to go into Genetics 101 but then realized it might be better not to "argue" with this powerful landowner.

This clinic continued for about twenty years, until it was no longer feasible due to staffing difficulties. After that, Wendy, our nurse from New Zealand, visited the Khan's family on occasion and carried on some of the Family Planning activities for long-time patients. The Khan's wife was not one of them!

MAHANDRI

WE HAD OCCASIONAL clinics in the Kaghan Valley at Mahandri, staying in the Government Rest House. Our team would go the afternoon before, so that people would know that we were there. Then we would see patients the next day. We used weekends for these trips when it was easier to get away from the hospital. There was no electricity, so we would set up to see patients on the verandah, where I would see up to 80 patients. In the meantime Ruth dispensed medicines and the DeHarts directed the patient flow.

One day I heard a lady asking her husband what the flowerpots were for. He explained to her that they were for flowers and just for decoration. She thought this very strange, as she had never seen one before. From way back in the hills reached only by footpath, she lived without any "frills" of any kind. At our noon break, I asked her if she had ever ridden in a motor vehicle. The answer was "No." When I asked if she wanted to ride in our VW van, she looked a bit dubious, but then did climb in between myself at the wheel and Ruth Arvidson on the other side. We took her down the road a mile or so and returned. When she got out, she innocently asked, "Where were the horses?"

SHARKOOL

A MONTHLY CLINIC was held at Sharkool rather regularly during the 80's. This was in another direction to the northwest, over some mountains on switch back roads and down into a broad plain. When we first started this clinic, we would set up at the Rest House, going the day before. The rest house was a little distance from the town of Battal, in a nice setting of trees in the plain. One month our team consisted of a young couple, Dave and Mary Davis (non medical), Jean Sodemann, a nurse, Laura a visiting medical student, and Rehmat our Bible woman. The team varied from month to month, according to who was available. Jean and Dave dispensed medicines from our van while I saw patients in a small room in back of the rest house. Mary directed the patient traffic, while Miss Rehmat talked to anyone interested about spiritual things. She also had Bible literature available for those who could read. We saw only 50 patients that first day, as word had not spread that we were present. Since we were done early, we drove into Battal to see some rather well off landowner friends who often came to our hospital.

We first stopped to see Bilqis, and found they were in the midst of wedding preparations for her brother's wedding. For this reason we were entertained at another relative's home who had had a baby at Bach two months previously. First we were served fruit and a rose-water drink, which is greatly relished by Pakistanis, but most foreigners find rather nauseating. Laura had never drunk or smelled it before, and she just could not manage it. Surreptitiously, we poured her glassful into mine, and I heroically managed to drink both. Our hosts thought we really liked it, and promptly refilled both glasses! But I could drink no more! We were then served a full "tea" of chicken, fries, pakordas (batter fried pieces of vegetable), and French toast. And, yes, there was plenty of tea to help wash down the food from the heavily laden table. At another house, we watched the wedding dancing and drumming (women only), and were shown the bride's gifts from the groom's family. She was richly outfitted with many suits of silken clothes and much gold jewelry which must have cost thousands of rupees amounting to more than most of their land tenants could make in a lifetime. In this home, one of their servants, Roshan Jan and her baby, came to see us. Her humble presence emphasized the difference in the social classes. (See the chapter on Lowly People)

The next day, we started clinic at 7 a.m. and had treated 110 people by 1 p.m. One might ask what is really accomplished by seeing so many patients in scattered areas periodically, with no good follow up. After all, most of them get worms again, and became anemic again, or whatever. Medically, perhaps we did not accomplish a great deal. We might pick up new TB patients who then could come to the hospital for regular treatment, or we might see a condition requiring surgery that could be referred to our hospital. There were always obstetric patients whom we could advise to deliver at the hospital because of some problem we detected. But more than the medical results, these clinics made for a lot of good will among the 99+% Muslim population in these areas. It got us out among the people on their home territory and not in the artificial hospital setting. We made a lot of friends, and were able to eventually see a few actually come to Christ after this initial contact. Dear Niamatullah (See Lowly People) first heard the Good News at the Oghi Clinic. A young man being trained for the Muslim priesthood came to the Sharkool clinic and obtained a Bible, leading later to his turning to Jesus for forgiveness of his sins and the assurance of his going to heaven.

After a few times having the Sharkool clinic in the government rest house, we were advised by local officials that we could no longer use it for that purpose. Someone must have objected to a Christian presence and reported it. We were able to rent a small building, which was out in the middle of a corn field. This was pretty primitive, but served our purpose except there was no bathroom! When the corn was cut, or not high enough to be private, we ladies would have no bathroom! We had to walk a distance to a mud dwelling where they let us use their facility in the courtyard.

Personally, I enjoyed getting away from the hospital routine and into the countryside. Although some trips were fraught with road problems, the gorgeous scenery of the mountains compensated, and the pastoral landscapes of planting and harvesting in the changing seasons were a delightful change. These clinics can no longer be held, due to staffing problems, and security reasons. This age of terrorism no longer allows the white foreigner to travel safely in these areas.

Trek To Quza Banda

10

One of the more pleasurable activities we enjoyed once in a while were treks north into the higher mountainous areas to visit hospital contacts. One of our favorite treks was to visit Quvvat Khan, the headman of Quza Banda. In May of 1971, we had a visiting ophthalmologist and his wife, Dr. and Mrs. Curtis Benton. The last couple of days they were with us we made such a trek. After finishing 20 cataract operations by noon, we left for the mountains. Climbing up the narrow road in our VW van, we reached the top of Susal Gali pass and started down. The scenery was all we desired for our visitors: the sun on the distant snow covered peaks, with dark rain clouds in the foreground, and hundreds of flooded rice paddies below. We arrived about 5 p.m. and immediately were given tea.

We took a walk around the flooded rice fields and saw a curious thing. A mother hen had been given duck eggs to hatch, and these little ducklings were frustrating her by sailing out on the shallow water in the flooded fields! Even with much clucking she was not able to keep them together on dry land. Margaret and I visited the inner courtyard and met the women of the family. Later we had supper with the men on the floor of the dried mud guest room. Curtis joined with Russ in eating with fingers, as is the custom, while we ladies opted for spoons. We slept in this same guest room on rope beds, after having made a trip to the orchard in the dark to attend to our personal needs. During the night we had a visitor—a rat!

The next morning we had breakfast with a nearby relative of Quvvat Khan. Aminullah's house was right next door to the village school, which was disrupted while the kids watched us eat! I saw several patients, even though I had sent word that this would not be a clinic trip. We visited the women's quarters again, where we had to have more eggs and tea. A poor servant lady was beseeching me to go see her daughter, in labor two days. As soon as we could leave the ladies, Margaret and I went into this dark nearby hovel. She had the experience of her life by assisting me deliver a fat baby girl with the aid of only two aspirin, some Wash and Dry towelettes, Russ's razor blade to cut the cord, and a piece of string to tie the cord, which she had pulled off the seam of her dress! She shined the flashlight for me and then took the baby in a scrap of cloth as big as a handkerchief, which was the only thing they could offer.

After this event, we trekked up the mountainside to Yousaf Khan's enclave, to see his two wives, mother and sister. More tea! Then we trekked on to Atta Mohd's village of Char Bagh, where we had a huge lunch. After we ate, Margaret and I visited the ladies. When we got back to the car, we found a huge clinic of women waiting. We had to disappoint them as there was no time. We did bring back a boy with a depressed skull fracture from a rock falling on him while he was riding in a jeep. Curtis and I made eye rounds at 6 p.m.! The Bentons could not get over their wild experiences in merged tribal area! They left for the USA the next morning. After clinic that day, I was able to take the skull fracture patient to surgery and elevate the pieces of skull. He made a full recovery!

11

The Low Born

THE LITTLE PEOPLE OF THE KINGDOM

James 2:5. "Listen, my dear brothers: Has not God chosen those who are poor in the eyes of the world to be rich in faith and to inherit the kingdom he promised those who love him?'

ROSHAN JAN

ROSHAN JAN CAME into the clinic one day as a lowly servant, accompanying the wives of some wealthy landowners from the village Battal. She was not registered as a patient herself. As I was doing pre-natal checks on the rich ladies, I noticed that she herself was large with child, and asked her employers if I could check her, too. The response was, "Oh, if you want to—but she doesn't have any money." She was very short of stature, and I knew she would have trouble delivering a child normally. We told her that she must come to the hospital to have her baby when her time came.

Shortly after that, on a cold, rainy day, Roshan Jan appeared absolutely alone with no money and just a little tin box containing her possessions. (All in-patients are expected to have at least one relative with them to feed and help care for them.) She was in labor, for which she needed a C. Section. Since she is somewhat slow mentally, no one cared for her in the village, not even her husband. Hospital staff fed her and cared for her and the new little baby boy. No one thought about what she might be learning in the ward devotions every morning, as she seemed too dull to understand. One day she told the evangelist, "I want to believe what you are telling about Jesus." What she understood, she accepted wholeheartedly.

We have visited her in her village, but the rich folks, who are also our patients, think it is SO strange that we want to visit such a lowly person! A couple of years later she had another C. Section with the same story repeated. No husband helped; no one accompanied her. She had a tubal ligation this time, after the birth of a daughter. This time she absorbed more of the Gospel story, as she listened daily in the ward. She was the only Christian in her village but continued as one of the "lowly people" in the Kingdom here on earth. She remained faithful until the Lord called her home to be rich in the Kingdom of Heaven.

PARI JAN

LUKE 21: 1-4 "As he looked up, Jesus saw the rich putting their gifts into the temple treasury. He also saw a poor widow put in two very small copper coins. 'I tell you the truth.' he said, 'this poor widow has put in more than all the others. All these people gave their gifts out of their wealth, but she out of her poverty put in all she had to live on'.

I know this widow. Her name is Pari Jan, and once or twice a year she comes limping down to the highway from her mountain village, boards a bus for a 2-3 hour bumpy ride to our hospital. She usually comes the afternoon before a women's clinic the following day. She comes directly to one of our homes, carrying her severely retarded albino child on one hip, and a chicken, or some eggs, shelled corn, or walnuts in a bag on her arm. She distributes her precious gifts, the widow's two mites, to her Christian friends on the hospital staff as her way of giving thanks to God for healing her and bringing her to know Jesus as her Savior. She has no temple treasury to give into, no church fellowship to worship with, so she brings her widow's mite to the only place where she knows there are any Christians, to our hospital. She stays overnight with one of our staff, or in the ward, finding delight in fellowship. The next morning she is at ward devotions, singing some of the songs she has learned and identifying herself with the believers. She goes over some of the verses she learned long ago as a patient. Since she is illiterate, this is the only Bible she has. Then she attends clinic for her medicine, and returns home. We will not see her again for 6 to 12 months, when she no doubt will again come limping in with her love gifts, her widow's mite.

This dear lady first came to the hospital years ago, scooting on the ground as she could not walk and had no crutches. Her right knee was contracted to a 90-degree angle from TB of the joint. It was swollen, draining pus, and she was in a great deal of pain. A 12-year old girl relative accompanied her to help her in the hospital and cook for her. Pari Jan was with us for many weeks while she received treatment, which was an operation to straighten and fuse her knee. With physiotherapy she learned to walk again. During this time she accepted the Lord and learned to love Him and memorize His word. Every time I see her coming to express her love and thanks to our Christian staff and to her Savior, I realize that I know the widow Jesus was talking about in Luke 11. She is another of the "lowly people" of the Kingdom. Isaiah 53:4 says, "Surely he took up our infirmities and carried our sorrows."

SAFIA

SAFIA, THE PARAPLEGIC/AMPUTEE returned to the hospital for a couple of weeks in 1988. She had hoped to find a place in St. Joseph's hospice in Pindi where they take chronic and handicapped people, but her mother decided she will not let her go there, even though her father and brother were willing. She cannot live any longer with her sister in Muzuffarabad in free Kashmir, as their house is already too crowded. She had been inside one room there for a year without ever seeing the sky, or a tree or flower, and no place for her wheel chair. She was just in bed. At the hospital, even though she was in a rather starkly furnished family quarter, she felt "liberated" as she could come in for ward preaching, wheel herself around the compound, and even visit us in our homes. She came to our house with an embroidered tablecloth she had been sewing for a week. Then her mother objected to her fellowship with Christians, and said she would take her home to the village beyond Muzuffarabad. The situation there is impossible. It is very inaccessible, and the family has many enemies in the village due to family troubles. But, praise God, her faith is so warm and radiant, in spite of her helpless and hopeless physical situation.

Niamatullah

JAMES 1:2-3, 5. "Consider it pure joy, my brothers, whenever you face trials of many kinds, because you know that the testing of your faith develops perseverance. If any of you lacks wisdom, he should ask God...."

Some years ago, dear Niamatullah had come to a hospital prayer meeting, looking so old and frail. He told us a wonderful miracle God had done for him. He is a peasant farmer way up beyond Oghi who has been the only believer in his village for many years. His only living son had taken Rs. 10,000 of the family savings and run away to Karachi 3 years previously. He had never come back. Niamatullah heard he had fallen into bad company, and finally decided to go to Karachi to look for him. Niamatullah was an old man, barely recovered from a mild stroke, and had never traveled that far (900 miles) or been to a big city before. He had no address, or any idea where to look for this son in a city of 10 million.

What a foolish, hopeless errand! He did go, and looked for days at bus stations, on the streets, in the bazaars with no particular plan. After about 20 days he was so discouraged he thought about walking to the seaside and just keep walking out into the water to end it all. But he prayed that God would help him in his desperate situation. That very day he saw his son on the street! They hugged each other; the son was forgiven and brought home to the village to be with the father again. He was so full of praise to God that night in prayer meeting, causing us all to rejoice with him. Now the son is the only Christian in his village, as his father has gone on to the Heavenly Kingdom. Another one of the "lowly people" now made rich!

12

High People—Significant Persons

$\mathcal{M}$ost of the people who come to Bach Christian Hospital are the poor, the insignificant, and the needy. They are the "real" people, with no pretense or airs of importance. They have raw needs, and are open and ready for help. On the other hand, sometimes there have also been rich, powerful, and politically important folks who have crossed our paths in one way or another. These are the people we would never have met in America. They were stimulating and challenging in a very different way.

INTRODUCTION TO THOSE OF THE UPPER ECHELONS

IN THE SPRING of 1958 Russ and I were invited to a tea in honor of the Prime Minister of Pakistan, Malik Sir Feroze Khan Noon. It was given in Abbottabad in a garden at the Army Officers Club, with a military band to furnish music. The Nowab of Amb, who was hosting the event, had invited us. He remembered my visits to his tiny kingdom to do pre-natal checks and deliveries for the Princess, his daughter-in-law. What a rare privilege for us neophyte, middle class, unimportant missionaries to be able to meet heads of the government of Pakistan! We enjoyed it thoroughly.

The next day the Nowab made an unexpected visit to our hospital, accompanied by three burly bodyguards armed with rifles, cartridge belts across their chests. I showed them through the hospital and wards, chatting in Urdu with the Nowab.

The next day I received an engraved invitation from the Health Minister of Pakistan to a breakfast in nearby Mansehra, in honor of the Prime Minister! This was held at the Government Rest House in

Mansehra, with a stunning view of the distant snowcapped Himalayas. It was a "durbar", or council, of many of the local village and clan chiefs. I also met a lot of "big wheels" such as the Food Minister, the Health Minister, and Lady Vicar-un-Nissa Noon, the British wife of the Prime Minister.

At that first meeting with Lady Noon, I was not impressed with her helpfulness. I used the occasion to ask for advice and help in getting a delayed shipment of much needed hospital supplies out of customs in Karachi. I remember her reply even after several decades, "My deaah, rules are rules, and that is that." I knew this was NOT true—there are many ways of influencing customs officials! Little did I know that she would later become a neighbor and really close friend with frequent contact over the years. She became very helpful to the hospital in several ways. However, that day I was glad to leave the presence of the high and mighty and get back to my needy patients! I will tell more about Feroze and Vicki in another chapter, and how they became "real" people to us.

Some time later we were invited to the home of the Commandant of the Pakistan Military Academy. This is Pakistan's equivalent of West Point. His wife was a patient of mine, hence the tea invitation. They had a lovely home, and were very friendly. Our outgoing Patty and smiling baby Nate made for immediate friendships.

Miriam, Sister-in-Law of the President

Sardar Bahadur Khan was the brother of the president of Pakistan, Ayub Kahn, and the head of the influential Muslim League. Ayub took over in a military coup in October, 1958. Sardar lived just a few miles from the hospital, in an imposing mansion set on a hill. I was called to this home one day, to see the mother of the President. The women, who were upstairs in the women's quarters, greeted me warmly. I was introduced to the old mother and shown her medical problem. She had a huge lipoma, a fatty tumor, on her lower back, and they wanted my opinion. I told them it was harmless, but could be surgically removed. Surprisingly, the old matriarch said, "No, thanks! It makes a good pillow for me when I sit!" They had no doubt gotten numerous opinions, and perhaps just wanted an occasion to meet the white lady doctor from the mission hospital. We had an elaborate tea before my departure.

The next time, I was called to see Sardar's wife, Begum Miriam. She was quite a character, village and uneducated, who liked to smoke her water pipe, the hooka. I took toddler Cindy along this time. She was undaunted by these important ladies who chucked her under the chin and stroked her attention-getting blonde hair. But when Miriam gave her a big pinch on the cheek, Cindy hollered, "Mutt karo!" I didn't know she even knew this phrase—a crude way of bluntly saying, "Don't do that!" I was mortified! Would we be thrown out of the country the next week for insulting the sister-in-law of the President? But Miriam had the opposite reaction. She laughed heartily at Cindy's spunk, and it made for a better friendship!

One evening the missionary staff from the hospital was invited to their home for dinner. We had a delicious Pakistani buffet downstairs with the men, and afterwards we ladies were invited to go upstairs and visit with Miriam and her daughter. They were in seclusion, or purdah, so do not go downstairs when men guests are present. I had a number of contacts with her over the years, usually as a patient. We dreaded to have her admitted as a patient, as she was so demanding. We had to humor her, cajole her, and try to keep her happy. Once she was in for hemorrhoid surgery, which the Lord enabled me to do successfully in spite of her high blood pressure. In a few days, she got so mad at our missionary Bible woman for sharing the Gospel with her that she was going to pack up and go home! I had to soothe her feelings, and she ended up reconciling with Merle and even kissing her! On one occasion we were able to give emergency treatment to Miriam for serious bleeding, and the family credited us with saving her life. This created a unique opportunity to get Christian literature into their home. The gifted and intelligent daughter showed great interest and read the Bible we were able to give her.

Mahmooda Salim Khan

Begum Mahmooda Salim Khan was a rich, influential lady from an important family. She was quite active in development programs to advance the welfare of the masses. We came to know each other through the Planned Parenthood Association, of which she was President, and through our mutual friend Lady Vicar-un-Nissa Noon. She was a most gracious and helpful lady and visited the hospital on special occasions. She was also the head of the TB Association of Pakistan and even arranged for the hospital to get free TB medicines for poor patients. I was a guest in her home at several meetings and other social events. She had an impressive cactus garden, from which she gave me some starts.

BILQIS SHEIKH

BILQIS SHEIKH WAS probably the richest, most well known Pakistani lady who has had a conversion experience to Christ. The fascinating story of her change is told in the book she wrote, "I Dared to Call Him Father." She was pointed to Jesus by a vision, not by any missionary, and was brought to Jesus through reading the Bible. She lived thirty miles or so from our hospital and was discipled by missionaries. We were in her home several times, but our most intimate relationship to her was many years later in Lahore. She returned as an old lady after a self-imposed exile in the USA for twenty some years, due to persecution. In Lahore, we lived close to her, and were in her home many times. She was a forceful, colorful personality who really loved the Lord. She was known as the "Flower Lady," since she had beautiful lawns filled with flower beds and flowering trees. She told us that she had made legal arrangements that upon her death she would be buried in a Christian cemetery, lest family would "reclaim" her for a Muslim burial. Dave and Synnove Mitchell, who had discipled her when she first became a Christian, were present as she was laid to rest in the Christian cemetery in Murree.

RETIRED NAVY COMMANDER

WE WERE INTRODUCED to the Afzal Khans by Lady Noon. They were neighbors to Vicki Noon and lived just down the road from our hospital. He was a former Naval Commander and then the head of Arbor Acres poultry farms. This was a project under the Ford Foundation and 52% owned by Nelson Rockefeller. From then on, invitations were often given to their home for dinners and teas. They also had a house in Nathia Gali, a resort area in the mountains. We always had our TEAM Annual Conference at a rustic hotel in Nathia. One year they invited the whole TEAM missionary family to their vacation house near the hotel for a big tea and coffee time. At another time, when Pakistan was at war with India, Afzal couldn't get enough chicken feed to feed their flocks; so they sent dozens of big, fat hens to distribute to all the hospital staff! The

Arbor Acres project introduced the chicken industry into Pakistan, and now there are similar chicken farms all over the country. When Bhutto came into power after that war, the Afzal Khans were under scrutiny by the C.I.D. (Pakistan's CIA) and accused of associating with Americans and therefore must be CIA agents.

Vicki Noon was also subject to questioning, and was called before the Governor of the Punjab and then Bhutto himself. She was relieved of her job as head of the Red Cross. She felt she was being left alone to "face the music" while the Afzal Khans quietly slipped out of the country via Kabul, Afghanistan, and eventually got to the USA. They took their six children, leaving behind their beautiful houses and gardens, and lucrative business. They became American citizens, but years later when the political winds changed, they returned to Pakistan. Sunny told us many amusing stories of her adjustment to America without all the servants she was accustomed to. One experience was putting way too much detergent in the washing machine and having to clean up all the suds—without the servants she was used to having in Pakistan. We continued our friendship for many years. She even attended Urdu services at the hospital chapel at times but never showed any serious consideration or understanding of the Gospel. We saw her one last time in 1998 on a return visit to Pakistan, when she was battling cancer and had already lost Afzal to a neurological disease. She still did not realize her need to have her sins forgiven.

THE AIR MARSHALL

WE MET ASGHAR Khan and his wife through Vicki Noon and the Afzal Khans. Asghar and Afzal were brothers. Asghar had been the former Air Marshall (head of the Air Force), and was a chief opposition to Bhutto. There were several attempts on his life by Bhutto's men of the Pakistan People's Party. We also met the son of former President Ayub, Gohar Ayub Khan, who was in politics himself. He lived only 10 miles from the hospital in Abbottabad. I remember at a dinner party at their house, when his gracious wife was serving the lady guests a special treat after a sumptuous meal. On a tray she had paan wrapped in betel nut leaves. Paan is powdered betel nut, a stimulant, and all I knew about it was that when men expectorated after chewing it, it made an ugly red splat on the pavement. I could hardly believe it was being served in this upper society group. When she came by my chair, she whispered, "I don't think you want any of this." I certainly did not, and was so grateful for her excusing me!

Some years later we were invited to their daughter's wedding. We were again at their large house in Abbottabad, but the festivities were held outside on the spacious lawns. We ladies were in back of the house in a very large open sided tent typically used for weddings, and the men were outside in another large tent. I really didn't know anyone there and was not completely comfortable. I did find out that she was marrying a cousin who was a cardiology resident in the United States! One doesn't really "see" the wedding, as there is no public ceremony. The Muslim cleric goes to the bride, and asks her if she is willing for this marriage. When she says yes, the men go to the mosque and conclude the contract. On return, the bride and groom finally see each other, and food is served.

Russ was sitting in the tent in front of the house with a visiting doctor from the USA. The family is all Pathan, an ethnic group known for their warrior traditions. The firing of high-powered guns is traditional to celebrate weddings, and the men guests were shooting up in the air into the trees. Russ was aghast to find out they were using live ammunition! He was sitting at the edge of the tent, near one of the gunmen. This man fired a loud shot just level with Russ's left ear a few feet away, which caused him intense pain. It did not rupture his eardrum as we feared, but he did lose most of the hearing in that ear. We finally were in our car, ready to leave. However, we couldn't get out of the driveway until another Pathan tradition was carried out. Right in front of the Mercedes Benz in which the bride and groom were leaving, a goat was slaughtered. We watched as the blood flowed across the driveway right in the path the car would take. As the car drove through the blood the couple was assured of being able to have children! This well ingrained tribal custom prevailed in spite of the groom's being a well-educated, American cardiologist.

A Bone to Pick

In the fall of 1972, one night very late, I had an unexpected encounter with the wife of the Spanish ambassador to Pakistan. We had just gotten home at 10:30 p.m. from a trip to Murree, and found that Dr. Hansmartin had two emergencies waiting for me. Vicki Noon had had a dinner party for some VIP's, and the Spanish ambassador's wife had swallowed a fish bone, which lodged in her esophagus. Vicki, Afzal and Sunny Khan had brought her to Bach Hospital, and all were slightly inebriated! I had never seen them in this condition, and if the medical situation had not been so serious, it would have been humorous! The patient was also somewhat tipsy, which helped relax her! I had to assemble the rarely used esophagascope while Dr. Hansmartin gave her Pentothal. (We read in the literature later that this anesthetic should not be used for head and neck procedures due to the possibility of laryngospasms, which cut off the breathing. The Lord surely sent some angels to protect!) I did pray as I put the long tube into her esophagus, as I was no expert in its use. I was able to snare the bone on the first try! Whew! After that I went on to the next emergency, which was an obstetrical one, the kind Dr. Hansmartin had not handled before. I was able to teach him on that case, and we finally finished at 1:00 a.m. Later, I received a handwritten note of appreciation from the Spanish lady who thanked me for removing her "bone of contention."

So what was accomplished by these social contacts with the "upper crust?" Probably not much in the spiritual realm. But several of them did get some exposure to the Good News, whether they heeded it or not. Our job is to be faithful, and God is responsible for the results! It did add some spice and diversion to our lives. At least two of these friends were able to help the hospital in various ways. They saw a difference in spirit between our hospital and the government institutions, a difference only Christ can make. We would never have met such people in America!

13

The Noons

SIR FEROZ KHAN NOON AND LADY VICAR-UN-NISSA NOON

*I*t is impossible in one chapter to capture the colorful, illustrious and fascinating characters of the Noons. We first met them in 1958, when he was the Prime Minister of Pakistan and she was the head of the Red Cross. (See chapter on Influential People) Feroz Khan Noon was born in a village of the Punjab, into a wealthy landowner family. He was educated at Oxford as a lawyer, and was prominent in the political life of India, and then Pakistan after it was formed. He held many offices and portfolios, including Indian representative in the British War Cabinet during WW II. He was High Commissioner (ambassador) from India to the U.K. He was the first Pakistani Governor of East Pakistan after the war (later in 1971 became Bangladesh), then Chief Minister of the Punjab before he became Prime Minister of West Pakistan. He had been knighted by the queen of England for meritorious services during WW II, hence the titles Sir and Lady.

Lady Noon was European by birth, and met Feroz in London, when he was High Commissioner for India in 1945. Years later, Feroz told me that when he had fallen in love with her, he had a Pakistani wife back in his home village along with several children. Some well-placed people advised him to "just take Vicki." He told me that that was against his moral code as a Muslim, but since Islam allows up to four wives, he decided to marry her! A beautiful and gracious lady, she was very active in humanitarian groups in both East Pakistan (now Bangladesh) and West Pakistan. She founded schools for women in both wings, which are still called by her name. She was the head of the Red Cross for about 20 years, then Minister of State for Tourism and later ambassador to Portugal. She was also active in other social service fields such as Child Welfare, Family Planning, and Drug Rehabilitation.

In addition, she was a great help to our hospital in the early years, helping us get a telephone exchange, the first in our area. She put pressure in the right places so that our missionary staff could get visas at a time when it was difficult, and gave substantial gifts at times for various building projects at Bach Christian Hospital. She often gave to the Charity Fund for poor patients. She became a close personal friend over the years.

We last saw her when we visited Pakistan in 1998 after our retirement. As we sat at tea in her home in Islamabad, Russ had a good chance to once again to present the Gospel. As far as we know, she never made a personal decision for Christ, but she had heard. She was a nominal Muslim from the time she married Feroz, but in theology was more of a Universalist. She was tolerant of all religions, and believed if you were good, that would give you hope of eternity. We received with real sadness the news of her death in 2000. Our son Nate informed us and told us he was able to go to her funeral.

So, how did we get to know the Noons? In the early 60's, after he had retired from government service, they established a summer home just about a mile from our hospital. They appeared at our door one day to ask if I would take Sir Feroz's blood pressure. We established a time when they could have this done regularly when they were in residence. Invitations to tea and dinners at their palatial residence followed. We sat out on their lawn for tea in good weather while Vicki's two black poodles cavorted around us. She was very fond of dogs, and since we are, too, we had a common bond! She liked our white Samoyed type dogs, and we took to her black poodles. The children often accompanied us, and I can remember Firoz's pleasure with our pre-school Cindy. He would entertain her, and as she was not abashed by his high position, she would respond. He told me one time while Vicki was not present, that she did not particularly like children—at least not close up! They did not have a family, but his village wife had borne him several children who were adults by the time we knew them.

Phyllis Irwin, M.D.

We often visited them at their home in Lahore 250 miles south of our hospital. We made yearly trips all that distance for dental work. I remember so clearly one visit when we arrived at their door for a dinner invitation, bringing all three children. It was just the natural thing for us to do; besides, we had no one to leave them with at the YMCA where we were staying.

When Lady Noon opened the door, for a brief moment I saw the abashed look on her face as she saw our kids. It vanished in a moment, and she hurriedly had three more places added to the long dining table set for many VIP guests! She was so gracious no one would guess that it was a real faux pas on our part to bring children! I have long since forgotten the important guests we met that evening, but I do remember what happened. Patty and Nate were really good throughout, but after the first course of soup, Cindy must have figured that was supper (as it often was in our home). She slipped down from her chair and spent the rest of the dinner hour playing under the table with the two poodles! Feroz got a kick out of that. I don't know what Vicki thought, but it did not stop the invitations!

Whenever they were in residence near us, we were always invited to tea or a dinner party. We continued to visit them in Lahore, and later, at her big home in Islamabad after Feroz was gone. He died of Parkinson's disease about 1970. We went through her distress during his illness, and at times were able to pray with her and encourage her from the Scriptures. She continued to be active for almost another thirty years. I think we saw more of her after his passing, as she was very lonely. On one visit she seemed depressed, and I was able to give her a copy of Good News for Modern Man.

She liked to paint as a hobby and has done some really nice watercolors. She liked gardens, and we would always "tour" her lawns while she frequently got plants and cut flowers from me at the hospital. Gardening was another common bond of our friendship. Once we attended a memorable dinner party at her house at which we met Gohar Ayub Khan, son of the former President Ayub and his wife, as well as retired generals and ambassadors. As we left, she gave me a sack to take home. She whispered, "It's a ham. Invite me when you have it for dinner!" Someone had brought it to her from overseas, but since Muslims are not to eat pork, she could not openly enjoy it. I enlisted the DeHart ladies, Garnett and Sarah, to help me plan and cook a meal worthy of a ham--and Vicki! The next Sunday DeHarts joined us for a big dinner with Vicki after church, and she dug in just like a member of the family!

One more vignette comes to mind. Once when Vicki was visiting us, she said she had never in her life been to a village but would like to do so. She had never learned Urdu fluently, either, as the elite crowds she moved in all spoke English. She could manage to talk with her servants, but could not really carry on a conversation in Urdu. We planned to take her on a village visit. Patty was home for the summer, and went with us. She drew the attention of everyone in the village, as she sipped tea along with the rest of us.

We drove her up to Bandi Dhundan, the nearest village where we had lots of friends. After jolting through the ruts and potholes, we parked and climbed the rough path to the village. Making our way along the narrow street (more like a path) we had to avoid the open sewage draining through from each courtyard. This unpleasant effluent flows through a hole in the wall, and joins the open drain in the middle of the path. We would hop from side to side to get the best footing. Nestling in the midst of the drain was a metal pipe, which brought fresh water from a spring above the village. One could only hope there were no leaks in the pipes! When we arrived at the door of the home where we were invited, we were greeted in the courtyard by a large gathering of people. Word had spread that this important lady was coming, and many of the village women had come to get a peek at her! They crowded around us, and children watched from the rooftop and over the courtyard wall. Although she was used to crowds, never had she been in one like this! We were served tea in this open area, rather than in the dark, windowless room that opened off the verandah. Lady Noon never asked to go "slumming" with us again!

I often wondered why she pursued our friendship, when she had so many other important friends and interests. She really seemed to enjoy our simple and sincere relationship. Perhaps it was because most of the time at her many dinner parties and social events, she had to put on her colorful "façade" for high society. When she was with us, she could just be her real self. The two facets of her personality were so evident. I liked the "vulnerable Vicki" better, when her real feelings were revealed. She could talk to us without restraint and with open heart. My regret is that she never seemed to understand her greatest need, which was that of a Savior.

Phyllis Irwin, M.D.

$$14$$

Kid Missionaries

$\mathcal{M}$y most important job as a missionary was to be a mom. When Russ and I first went to Pakistan, our first child, Patty, was a year old. In fact, she had her first birthday on board ship in the Atlantic. She took her first steps in a hotel in Rome, and learned to walk on board ship in the Mediterranean. Young parents today looking to the mission field have many questions and concerns about their children: schooling, health, environment, and even emotional needs. Some are hesitant because of what they think are the "risks."

As we look back 40 years on rearing our 3 children in Pakistan, we just want to say, "It was worth it all." I like what I heard recently—our kids were not just Missionary Kids, but Kid Missionaries. A Christian family model in a foreign culture is one of the best ways to portray the life of Jesus Christ. It opens opportunities for presenting the Gospel. Babies and young children "break the ice" more quickly than adults. Who can resist the smile of a baby, the antics of a toddler?

Our first trek as a family to a mountain village in Free Kashmir was to visit an out-patient clinic contact. We drove as far as we could. Our host met us with a horse, which was for baby Nathan (8 months old) and myself. The others walked the hour or two over the rocky path to the village. Everybody came out to look at the white family with a baby and a toddler. They couldn't believe we would come all that way just to visit them. Naively, we had not come prepared to stay all night, but soon realized that it would be impossible to get back the same day. I didn't have enough diapers for Nate, and he developed diarrhea while we were there. No Pampers available! The host's young son gladly took the soiled cloth diapers and rinsed them in the nearby stream, solving that problem. But this was the same stream where they got their drinking water! The boiled water we had brought was saved for our kids. As the hot afternoon and our thirst advanced, Russ and I decided to drink their water. Reasoning? It was better to die of typhoid later than to die there of dehydration! Actually neither situation materialized. We had a great time with this family, and our kids were really KM's, making friends and opening hearts. Our 2½ yr old Patty had brought a small rubber doll with her, with moveable eyes. That was the ultimate for the village kids! They had never seen anything like it!

When it was time to go, my Pakistani clinic helper who had gone with us told me that it would be fitting if we gave the doll to the host's children, since they had been admiring it so. Culture dictates that whatever is admired by a guest is to be given to him. I had learned this early on, on my first visit to a Pakistani home. Trying to make conversation in my very limited, newly learned Urdu, I admired the tablecloth. The hostess promptly took it off the table and gave it to me! But now, WHAT TO DO? How would Patty react to giving her precious doll away? How could we not do it and violate the unspoken rules of the culture and possibly stunt our budding friendship with this Muslim family? Well, Patty was a true KM. She did not put up a fuss at all. The doll was given, a friendship was deepened, a contact and witness maintained.

PATTY AS A KID MISSIONARY

WHEN PATTY WAS about 7 years old, home on vacation from boarding school, she took it upon herself to entertain a Pakistani drug company representative who was waiting on our front porch until I returned at noon from the hospital clinic. (Our homes and hospital buildings were all on the same compound.) She engaged him in conversation. Some time later, he told me Patty had been telling him about Jesus! He was impressed.

CINDY AS A KID MISSIONARY

A FEW YEARS later, when our third child Cindy was a pre-schooler and the other two were off in boarding school, we took her on trek with us. She crossed a tributary of the Indus on the shoulders of a Pakistani guide as we went to visit patient contacts in Tribal Territory. Another time Cindy went with me by jeep late at night with six armed bodyguards to see an old village chief we knew who had had a stroke. The family insisted that the Doctor Mem Sahiba come see him right away. Were we safe? Certainly! No one would harm us with a small child along.

Patty went with me regularly to out patient clinics in Azad (Free) Kashmir, sharing the adventure of getting stranded driving through a rising river and having to be carried to shore while the hapless VW van remained stuck. Cindy accompanied me to monthly clinics over the Susal Gali pass to Oghi, also getting stuck in a river once. We took all the children to nearby villages, eating and drinking what was offered. They loved it! All 3 kids watched me do surgery and the girls observed deliveries from time to time. I remember the first time Cindy watched me do a bladder stone removal—she must have been about 5. When I held up the stone, she said from her perch on the sidelines, "Mommy, who threw that stone in the boy's tummy?"

When the kids were older, they worked at the hospital as "aides" during their vacations from boarding school. They were thrilled to be called "doctor" by most of the patients! By being a part of their parents' work from the beginning, by being included, they never felt like they were a burden that we had to pack off to boarding school so we could do "ministry." We made the most of times at home when they were out of boarding. Although I maintained a full hospital schedule, we could still do simple things, such as an evening walk, or play soccer in the side yard, or have a picnic by the nearby stream, or an overnight in a rest house up in the mountains. We were always amazed how little it took to entertain them. No TV, no movies, no CD players, no expensive toys. But enjoyable family times, meaningful tasks, good books, and family devotions more than made up for what they didn't have.

After college, Patty came back out for a year to serve as a boarding mother for little girls at our MK school. Nate came one summer during college to do an anthropology project, which involved visiting villages, mosques and holy graves. Cindy returned for a six months short term of Teaching English to Afghan refugees. So it is not surprising that Patty became a missionary to the Philippines; that Nate became the principal of our Bible Institute; and that Cindy is in Pakistan, having terrific opportunities to disciple new Afghan refugee believers through contacts of the ESL program.

So, young parents, do not hesitate going to the mission field because of your young children. What an exciting opportunity to see God work! Grandparents, do not be anxious or fearful for your son or daughter to go abroad with your precious grandchildren. God has a great plan for them, and He will take care of them as He knows best. After all, the safest place to be is in the center of God's will. Find out what He wants you to do, where He wants you to go, and step out in faith, being confident of this, that "He who began a good work in you will carry it on to completion until the day of Christ Jesus." And, you who stay home, pray for Missionary Parents, that they will have the parenting skills and discretion in decision-making they need in a different culture. Pray for MKs to be KMs, who might one day reach out to their friends of a different language and background. Pray for their adjustment to schooling, whatever that may be in a particular situation. Pray for transition when they return to USA for college. This is probably the greatest adjustment MKs have to make.

For us, was it worth it all—the hardships, the bouts of amebic dysentery, the hepatitis, boarding school, the frequent good-byes and separations? This Missionary Mom says an emphatic "Yes, it WAS worth it all!" If we had it to do over again, we would follow the same path. It is not that we did everything right, because we made mistakes. It was because He does not make mistakes, and He is the one in charge. Let Him take charge of your life, of your family. Then we, and you, can say with John in III John, "I have no greater joy than to hear that my children are walking in the truth."

15

Orphans

Our first "orphan" was brought to us very shortly after we moved to the hospital. The mother died in childbirth just across the road, from hemorrhage of a retained placenta. They would not bring her to the hospital for treatment. A day or so later, the family brought the wee four pound girl to us since they had no way of taking care of her. Because we had no nursery or staff to care for it in our hospital (we didn't even have a ward yet!), we took it to our home on a temporary basis. We taught the paternal grandmother to bottle feed, using clean but not fully sterile technique. After a few weeks, the baby went home and we were able to check on her periodically. Later the maternal grandmother, who was ignorant of basic hygiene, came from Lahore and took her to the big city far south of us. Patty and Nate were sad to see her leave. We visited her once in Lahore and realized that she would not survive long in that environment. After a few weeks the baby died of diarrhea.

There followed a succession of needy babies in our home. One was a wee preemie, born to a cachectic, paraplegic mother with huge bedsores. The mother died shortly after delivery, and the family had no way of caring for the tiny infant. I dropper fed it in our home for a while, but it was hard to fit that in with a full hospital schedule. This baby also did not survive long after it returned home.

Even later when we had hospital facilities to care for orphan newborns, some were brought to us at an older age. We still had no way to care for them except in our home. One precious little girl several months old was brought to us by her grandfather. He tried to care for her after the mother died, but found he could not cope. He had tears in his eyes as he put her into my arms and gave me a small bag of her clothing. Our children were home from boarding that winter, and they became greatly attached as they helped care for her. We found a Christian home for her in Malakand district, and were able to get news of her occasionally as she thrived with her adoptive family.

One day a newborn baby was brought to us by our hospital clerk, Allah Dad Khan. As he was walking to work, he crossed a small bridge over a dry stream bed. He heard a faint crying in the streambed. He wondered if it could be an animal, but when he went to investigate, he found a newborn female infant wrapped in a blanket. He brought it along with him to the hospital. Allah Dad was a Muslim, and since he had found the baby, we knew we would have to find a Muslim family. It was our practice to adopt babies into Christian families. It so happened that on our list of applicants for adoption, we did have a Muslim. He was the cook for one of our missionary nurses and was childless. We couldn't tell him outright that he would not be acceptable by reason of being a Muslim, so his name was added to the list. Now seemed to be the time God arranged. Jinda and his wife were thrilled to have Noreen in their home. They lived on the hospital compound, so the child was often in Ruth's home where her daddy worked. She attended Sunday School that Ruth held weekly for the compound children where she learned many Bible stories. She was able to go to a local girls' school and get a basic education.

Phyllis Irwin, M.D.

One baby girl was adopted by Dr. Money, who at that time worked part time in our clinic. She and Walter were Christians from nearby Abbottabad, and Rhuma became their much loved daughter. She attended the MK school in Murree where our children had gone. She is now a teacher in a private school in Abbottabad.

Some of our babies went to missionary families, although it was very difficult to accomplish the red tape required for taking such children out of the country. Laura went to the Innigers. Beate was adopted by German missionaries, Dr. Hansmartin and Thekla Killguss. Both girls also attended the MK school in Murree. Other orphans were taken to Sweden. Patty and I were able to visit one of these in her new family when we were on a trip to the States. An interesting observation is that all three of these families later had biological children of their own, after having been unable to conceive before! There must be something about those "Bach babies!"

One orphan, Arif, was 8 years old when he came to the hospital with his grandmother. She was terminal with tuberculosis and knew she was going to die. She had no one to take the boy, so her last hope was to give him to the hospital. Before she died, she signed him over to the hospital in the presence of a magistrate to be raised a Christian. We enrolled him in our Abbottabad Christian School. He had never been in school before, but soon was sixth in a class of forty! It was difficult to adopt out an older child, but God provided an older childless Christian couple in Tarbela who took him as their son. The day he left was a sad one for our staff who had been so helpful to him. Some of them cried; I cried, and even Arif cried. But all felt this was God's arrangement, as he really needed a home.

Another unadoptable baby was found on the hospital grounds by one of the watchmen, but no one saw who had left it. The newborn boy was a microcephalic and would never be normal mentally. Yet the Lord even provided for this child by a German pastor and his wife who were looking for a handicapped child to adopt. They came from Germany to receive him into their home!

An unusual circumstance developed when a female baby was "left over" at the end of a clinic day. The last patient to be seen said she had been holding this baby for someone while they went in to see the doctor. She had no idea to whom it belonged, as it had been passed around for some hours among the waiting patients! So this precious life was taken to our nursery to be cared for until she was adopted.

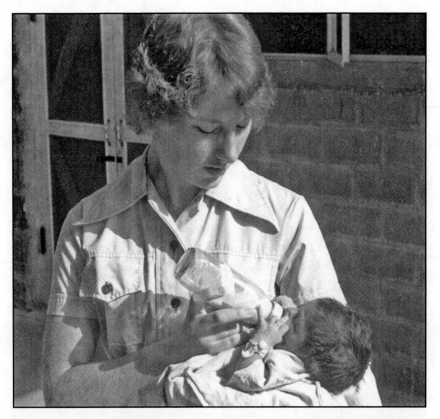

Most of our Bach "orphans" were born to unmarried mothers. While most such pregnancies end in illegal abortions by village midwives, those who carry to term are offered delivery at our hospital and the babies are signed over to us. It is such a deep family disgrace for this sort of thing to happen that most Muslim families quietly kill both the mother and the unborn child. They are often poisoned, or killed by their brothers. So our Bach Babies are extremely blessed to have the gift of life itself. Most are also blessed to have Christian parents. This compassionate ministry still goes on, and we have Bach Babies all over the western world as well as in Pakistan.

16

Village Trekking

During the fall harvest season the clinics are not as crowded, and it was a good time to plan treks, as long as the hospital work was covered. In the fall of 1970, Wendy, an RN from New Zealand and I met that intrepid trekker couple, Jack and Elma Ringer, at Oghi. We set out from there. We walked about an hour from the Oghi Fort (the last outpost of the British on the edge of tribal territory) to Niamatullah's village. He is a poor farmer who came to faith at the Oghi Clinic through Jack. His simple faith was an inspiration to us all. (See Chapter on The Little People.")

His village of Dewal was very poor, dirty, and backward. Filthy kids came flocking out to see us. Chickens were scratching here and there. Our host had only one room in his house, so we were entertained in the "village guest room." After tea, we saw our first patients. Then we ladies took a walk around the village and sat with several women in their miserable homes. We were able to give the Gospel to some. We visited Niamatullah's shop, which was a tiny hole in the wall. After the evening meal, we had a worship time with our host and his family. Villagers kept coming in and out, to listen or just to stare at the foreigners! Finally, after dark, we were able to make our trip to the "cornfield latrine" before settling down for the night.

At 6 AM water was brought to our room in a pitcher for our morning ablutions. After breakfast of tea, eggs, and paratas brought by Niamatullah's wife, we started seeing patients again. Our host's wife was one of the first patients, and I was aghast to find that she had TB! Everyone in the village has tapeworm! In fact, as we were sitting drinking tea, I was startled to see a chicken scratching nearby find a segment of tapeworm and gobble it down! A child had apparently squatted there and left the deposit. I confess, that was a bit revolting!

As we walked to another village, we watched the men at harvest, treading out the rice with oxen and then winnowing it by hand. After walking about a mile we reached another village where we saw a lot of patients, after tea, of course! That is customary protocol. We then walked about an hour past a series of water mills in a stream to a lovely village on a cliff just above the water. This village, Trourda, was much cleaner. What made the difference? Maybe it was the proximity of water. Each of these small villages seems to have a common guest room for the use of anyone fortunate to have guests. We had the usual tea in the men's guest room with Jack, and then were taken inside a courtyard to the women's guest room. Always the segregation! We saw several patients there, even after dark by the light of a lantern. There is no electricity in the whole area. After supper in the men's guest room, we had a great meeting with a bunch of eager school boys. We taught them two Bible choruses in Urdu, which they sang enthusiastically. I told them a Bible story, with pictures.

We felt privileged the next morning to get warm water in the pitcher! We had a day of more patients in several places, more tea, eggs and paratas, and several good chances to share the Gospel.

Our next stop was Dilbori, a large village on the main road, which we reached in the VW. The room in the bazaar we were first given to hold clinic was horrible, and we asked for a change. We moved to a house where it was much cleaner, and where we saw patients until after dark. We were in the battack, a room in larger homes where the men entertain male guests. It is accessible from the street, not through a courtyard, so that ladies remain separate. A khan who wanted us to see his women the next day sent a huge supper. Then we ladies went to the women's quarters where we saw several patients of the household. We were overnight there, listening to the mice play all night, while Jack was in the battack.

The next morning we proceeded to the khan's home where we saw many patients, including one really sick baby. Most of the women were not really sick. They just wanted attention. Since most could profit by worm treatment, iron pills and vitamins, we could satisfy them. Later in the day, when we got back to Oghi, it almost looked like civilization! It was good to get home that evening and enjoy a hot bath!!

17

Hippies And Helpers

*D*uring the late 60's and 70's, when the hippie movement was in full swing, we frequently got world travelers who drifted by the hospital on their way north to the beautiful Kaghan Valley. We were not on the "main route", which was Kabul, Afghanistan to Delhi, India, to Kathmandu, Nepal, where cheap hashish and morphine were readily available. But some wandered north past Bach Hospital and, at times, would show up in the clinic with hepatitis or dysentery. We finally set aside a family quarter for these sick ones, and I found some old pans, dishes, and a camp stove which we loaned to them for cooking. It would usually be a guy and a gal, and the one who was not sick would care for the other one.

One who came several times was John, a young man from Denmark. He came alone one spring with hepatitis. In the fall, he returned after having been in India and was on his way home to Denmark. The next spring he came with a girl friend, Karen. She had had hepatitis in India. They came on Sunday, and attended Sunday School at the chapel. Russ taught in both Urdu and English, for their benefit. They also attended Urdu service. They had lunch with us before leaving and then returned for the evening English service. They certainly seemed interested even though they had studied Buddhism in India the last six months. They kept seeking, but never finding, and wandered the world to try to find peace with God.

One day in clinic a Mexican-American from California showed up with tummy troubles. His name was Michael, and he was in his third year of working his way around the world as a carpenter and painter. We invited him to our house for supper. Our children were home from boarding and found him very interesting, as he was into yoga. We talked to him until late at night, and the next day one of our menial staff took him home for supper, so concerned that he would become a believer in Christ. He stayed in the ward while his lab tests were being done, and then stayed on doing little jobs. We gave him a temporary job painting in the chapel, and assigned him a room to stay in. He had daily talks with one or another of the staff, and spent hours discussing the Bible with Russ. He was often at our house for meals and came to the Sunday evening English services. He even joined in prayer, but really seemed mixed up with his yoga philosophy.

Patty had long talks with him at our home, and at times would get so frustrated with his reasoning! He stayed for several months. One evening we were having family devotions, and the children were praying for his salvation. Just then, he knocked at the front door and he told us he had just accepted the Lord! What an answer to prayer that was for them! He said, "That was the easiest way to 'pass the buck' I've found!"

The next day he said he wanted to be baptized, and started studying the Bible with joy. Patty, Nate, and even Cindy could answer his many questions about the Bible. He stayed on, living with us and attending all meetings. He was baptized in the wading pool next door, along with Bruce Rasmussen. Russ conducted the service both in English and Urdu, as many of our staff were well acquainted with him and were rejoicing that he had become a believer. A couple of weeks after that, he left saying he would attend the winter camp for MK's (Missionary Kids) to be held in about a week in Taxila. He did not show up there, and we lost track of him. Was he a true believer? I'm glad God is the one who knows the heart! We did our part!

Bert and Hillary were from Australia, on their way around the world. They were on a bus headed for the Kaghan when our Pakistani lab director, Nathaniel, happened to meet them. He graciously invited them to stop at the hospital overnight and had them at his house for supper. Sort of puzzled as to how to entertain them, he took them to Dave and Synnove Mitchell. Soon Dave came to get us to come meet them.

What an interesting couple! She was the daughter of the Australian ambassador to France, and Bert an accomplished violinist who had been with the Chicago Philharmonic Orchestra. He took his violin with him everywhere. Soon we were enjoying an impromptu concert, with Russ at the piano, Bert on the violin, and Synnove singing. Hillary also had a beautiful voice, and we still remember the haunting strains of "Indian Love Call" that she and Bert performed. The conversation turned to spiritual things, and Bert eagerly asked questions. The discussion continued until nearly midnight, when Russ suggested an adjournment as several had to be at work at the hospital early the next morning. Bert pleaded, "But only if you will talk to me again in the morning!"

Next day they did talk, all morning, while Synnove talked with Hilliary. Russ urged Bert to accept the Lord, as he seemed to really understand. However, they left that afternoon on the bus for the Kaghan without making a decision. We had offered to keep his violin until they returned, but he decided to take it with them.

About a week later they returned, and Bert told us he had accepted the Lord on the bus a few minutes after they had left the hospital! He said that he was under deep conviction, and he knew he should give his heart to the Lord. His palms were sweaty as he struggled. Then he said, "I did it!" He had read all the "assignments" Russ had given him and was eager for more. They were with us for supper, and we enjoyed some good violin and piano music. Bert said the violin came in handy for making friends up in the Kaghan Valley, as they sat in the tiny tea shops.

They couldn't speak Urdu, but he would play the violin and men and kids flocked to watch and listen. Often the shopkeeper would not charge them! They stayed with us for several days and became part of the family! Hill, an expert seamstress, finished a blue dress I was working on for Cindy. When we four got into a discussion about prophecy, even Hill was interested. She maintained, however, that Bert in his naivety would soon lose his enthusiasm for his new beliefs. They were headed for India, and then Nepal, where we suggested they stay at the Dil Aram house in Kathmandu. The name means "heart rest", the place established for world travelers and hippies who needed help and a place to stay. There were regular Bible studies and fellowship with believers. Bert said he would write to us from there, but only after Hillary had accepted the Lord. He was sure she would!

We did not hear for many weeks. We wondered if they had dropped out of contact as most of the other world travelers had. Then one day we received a letter from Bert with the good news! Hillary had become a Christian! They were headed home to Australia to get married and go to Bible College. Wow! They did follow through, prepared for ministry and are still serving the Lord in Australia! We still hear from them at least yearly, and it is so good to know they are "fruit that abides."

In contrast to the vast majority of drifters, the restless world traveler type of visitor, we had a steady stream of focused, purposeful young people who came to our hospital. These were the medical students, who come in their senior year on a third world medicine rotation from their medical schools. They were from the USA, Canada or UK, and spend two to three months working with the doctors on the wards, in the clinics, and in surgery. They lived in our home, or with another missionary family, as we had no guest facilities in the hospital. They rotated among our homes for meals; so we really got to know them. Later the hospital had adequate housing facilities; so the students were more on their own.

It actually slowed down the work to have a student alongside. In the clinic, translation was necessary for them to understand what the patient and the doctor were saying. It also took time to explain what we were doing and why we made a certain diagnosis and treatment plan. It took longer in surgery to let them close after an operation, but actual suturing was an important part of their training. It was enjoyable and rewarding as they learned certain skills. They saw conditions and diseases they would not see in a modern, western medical setting. By the end of their stay, they were actually becoming good helpers, and we missed them when they were gone. Most of these young people were Christians, some seeking God's will in their lives for overseas service. We saw three of these medical students return to Pakistan to work in various mission hospitals. It was our pleasure to visit two of these in hospitals in the southern province of Sindh during our last term.

One of these students was Bill McKelvey, married to a nurse named Shiela. They were coming to Pakistan from Newfoundland in Canada at a time when I was returning from a trip to the States. We made arrangements to meet in Heathrow airport in London. I had never met them and had not even seen a picture of them. As I walked through the huge waiting lounge, I wondered how I would recognize them. I found a couple dozing on each others' shoulders, with an open Bible on the small table in front of them. Aha! I sat down quietly next to them, and when they stirred after a while, I asked if they were the McKelveys. They were! We began to get acquainted on the rest of the journey to Bach Hospital. During the months they were with us, I learned to really appreciate them and their desire to serve the Lord. During our last term in Pakistan before we retired, I was helping out at the Kunri Hospital in the Sindh where they had been posted for some years. It was a pleasure to be in their home, see their young children, and help Bill in the medical work.

Priscilla was a good, steady help when she was with us at Bach Christian Hospital. At that time she did not indicate a strong leading to return as a career missionary doctor, but years later we heard that she and her family were posted at the Baptist Hospital in Shikarpur. Our last term I filled in at this hospital for a short time, and I was thrilled to meet her again. She was the only doctor there, valiantly carrying a heavy load. I could empathize with her from my early years at Bach!

Most of these students settled into medical practice in their home countries, but their third world experience helped them have a larger world view and realize God's heart for reaching all people. They could better pray for missionaries and encourage the mission effort. A number of these are still in contact with us.

Ingrid Mason Mail is an internist, attending our home church so we see her regularly. Janet White, now an ophthalmologist, keeps us up on her family and practice location. Martha Twaddle was delightful and humorous, besides being an excellent student. We were able to attend her wedding near Chicago when we were in the USA. She went into geriatric practice, and is now in hospice care. We lost contact with Abe Taves, but always remember his ability to walk on his hands! He was six feet six inches tall. He would entertain our kids. One time when he was on a trek with us, he amazed the village folks by walking on his hands on the far side of our VW van so that they could only see his feet "walking" in the air!

There were many other students throughout the years, and we found them all real helpers, a breath of fresh air from the west, and a joy to work with. We just included them in our family life, took them on picnics, village treks, to archeological sites, and to out clinics. We could wish that our hippie friends, who never found what they were seeking, could have been as settled and focused as these helpers. What a difference God makes in our lives!

Phyllis Irwin, M.D.

18

Concerning Chitral

FLIGHT FIZZLES - JARRING JEEP JOURNEY

The tiny kingdom of Chitral is isolated and inaccessible. It borders Afghanistan on the west and is nestled in the Himalayas. It is towered over by mighty peak of Tirich Mir (25,230 ft). The only way in is by air and one unpaved road, if the weather is good.

Our medical team was anxious to make a return visit after the only doctor there invited us back to hold clinics again. Irene, Wendy and I set off very early the morning of October 8, 1971, for Peshawar to meet the Ringers. We actually boarded the plane for our forty-minute flight, with an "Insha Allah" (If God wills) by the stewardess. The scenery was just getting spectacular when the plane turned around and headed back to Peshawar! "Technical Failure" we were told. No more flights for four days. We engaged an ancient Chevy "taxi" to take us to Dir state. The long, torturous road took us through Mardan and Malakand to Dir. We had a flat tire in Tukht Bhai, which the driver had fixed in that frontier village. During the break we had chicken curry at a "greasy spoon." By now it was well after dark.

We still had the long mountain road to traverse at 5-10 miles an hour, arriving in Dir city about midnight. Jack Ringer with difficulty aroused an innkeeper who made room for us in his minus five star hotel. The innkeeper had to rouse five men from their beds in a room for eight, and sent them out to sleep in the courtyard. We were given their beds, including their pre-warmed greasy bedrolls. After the eviction there were only three remaining men with whom we shared the room. No use being squeamish at midnight in a wild, frontier village! We did ask the man where we could relieve ourselves, a task that was quite urgent after the long ride. He looked at us women, puzzled, not being used to this gender at his establishment! Then he gave two options: Outside the courtyard in the unpaved street (after all, it was pitch dark and no one about!), or on the mud rooftop over our sleeping room. We opted for the latter, climbing a rickety wooden ladder leaning against the wall. But what would we do in the morning light? Either spot would be quite visible! No use worrying at that time when we were so tired that the dirty beds actually seemed inviting! We dropped, exhausted, and all was quiet.

Sometime in the wee hours we heard Irene scream in English, "There's a man trying to get in my bed!" One of the three men guests in our room had to go outside. On return he was confused in the dark as to which rope bed charpai was his. After apologies and sorting out of beds, we settled down again. I was absolutely shocked the next morning as we laughingly discussed this event to hear our staid, prim sixty-ish New Zealander Alma Ringer say to our Swedish single lady, "Irene, you missed the chance of a lifetime!"

In the morning we found there were forty or more men sleeping all over the veranda, courtyard and other rooms, so we ladies deferred our bathroom options, and stayed right in our beds while we were served tea. Later, while Jack was arranging a jeep, we took a walk and found a stream nearby which served as our flush! We even had time to visit the

Civil Hospital, which was a fairly nice building, but without a doctor, equipment or medicines!

We set off with nine people and mounds of baggage. One passenger (all men, of course), managed to sit on a bag in which he felt the point of Alma's bread knife. Unknowingly, he even ground our medicines from pills to powders! We stopped short of the Lowry Top (the pass into Chitral) for tea, and I had them boil the eggs I had received in Dir for seeing a patient. Up, up, over the 13,000 foot pass and down the torturous switch-backs, backing up on some of them to make it around. The dust was terrible, tinting us a light brown to match the local populace. We arrived at Darosh mid afternoon. While we waited for a cup of tea, our host, Dr. Sardar, appeared. He has been transferred to Darosh and arranged for us to stay there for a few days. He took us to his ancestral home nearby, where we washed up and had a nap. He is of royal descent, so his home, an old dwelling with past elegance, was rather posh for this area. We ladies had supper with his wife and other female relatives and gratefully went to bed.

After breakfast in the guest quarters, we met the doctor's father, who at that time was next in line to be the ruler as he was "Prince #1." Jack had a long chat with him in Pushto, with an exposition of Romans 1. He had read all of "Good News for Modern Man" that we left with him last year.

Later Dr. Sardar took us for a tour of the Health Center where we had ladies clinic the next day in a very small room. We ladies spent the afternoon in the harem with the women, learning some Chitrali medical phrases to use in clinic. We had to work through English, Urdu and Pushto. It was also a good witness opportunity. Later Dr. Sardar took us to tea at the home of a Captain of the Chitral Scouts.There I did a pregnancy check on his young wife. They are Punjabis and very unhappy in Chitral. We then visited the road engineer who is a Pathan, to do a similar check for his wife and drink more tea! Finally back to the big house to check Dr. Sardar's wife, who is also pregnant!

Medical Ministry to Many

Our three nurses and I opened clinic in one small room. Women and children crowded into the space in almost unmanageable numbers. To be seen by a woman doctor was something they had never experienced in Chitral before. Medical care there is rudimentary and primitive at best, but mostly non-existent. Three days and 400 patients later we moved by jeep farther up the lovely valley to the city-village of Chitral, the capitol, where the majestic snow-crowned Tirich Mir dominates the scenery. Here we worked at the small government hospital with its staff composed only of medical aides. There were no doctors or nurses.

In these limited facilities we saw some 200 patients. Wendy dispensed our own medicines, as they have <u>nothing</u> in the hospital, not a bandage or a cotton ball, nor any medicines or equipment. One young patient I saw was eight years old and had been married for six months! Dr. Sardar told us it is the usual custom. His older brother and his wife were both five when they were married! Women often do not remember their own names, as after they have a son, they are known only as "Sultan's mother!"

One day we were awakened with an earthquake at 3 a.m.! The next night another shock came that caused the hotel to shake and creak. It made us feel vulnerable and uneasy on the second floor.

Royal Regent Revisited

A highlight was the invitation we ladies had to the palace to visit the Mehtar's mother, the acting "Queen Mother." She is the sister of my old friend and patient, the Princess of Amb. Stepping through the crumbling archway into the palace grounds was like stepping back in time. The falconry was located in this entry, with rows and rows of young captured falcons sitting hooded on their perches ready to be trained for the hunt. Inside, a big lunch was served on the floor on the Persian carpets. The ruler and six teen-age girls who are relatives she cares for, ate with us. She showed us photo albums, including a couple of pictures of Patty, Nate, and myself when we were in Shergarh visiting the Princess some years before! She took us through all the old, unused parts of the palace. We had tea in a gilt and mirrored hall used for male guests long ago. She showed me a book, "Pilgrim's Progress" which I had given to the Princess of Amb when I was there for a delivery. Later, after the Princess died, she took the book to read herself. Only God knows the ripple effect it might have!

STRANGE SOCIETY SCRUTINIZED

A JEEP TOOK us to Ayun village, where we joined the road engineer and three other officials, for a trip into Bumboret, one of the three kafir ("infidel") valleys snaking very near the border of Afghanistan. After five more miles in the jeep, the road ended and we started climbing a steep mountain. Jack was puffing, with his bad hip causing him to limp, but he would not be dissuaded. After an hour or so, we reached the top and beheld the gorgeous Bumboret and Rumbur valleys. Then it was DOWN for several hours. In some ways this was even harder to traverse. Mid afternoon we got down to stream level where we gratefully splashed our hands and feet. How tempting to drink of the crystal clear water, but we dared not! We had seen how many of the villages in the main valley had latrines in their homes built right over the stream for instant flush! Jack was bushed, and when offered beer which the men had brought, he said, "It's medicine!"

The valley was beautiful with yellowing mulberry trees, great walnut trees, and pastoral scenes of sheep in quiet fields with water courses running everywhere. In late afternoon we reached a "dispensary" and were revived with tea, eggs, and paratas, a type of bread. This was our first food all day, except for pomegranates. Jack and Elma decided to stay there, as they could not push farther. Irene, Wendy and I continued on with the four Pakistani men. We pushed on through several Kafir villages with their strange architecture of wooden log dwellings to the end of the line--a small government rest house with a lone watchman to see to our needs. We roasted hunks of rib and liver on skewers over the open fire in the fireplace, which furnished the only lighting. Strange, indeed, for three white women to be tucked away at the end of the world in a weird culture, with men we did not know! I'm sure the angels were on duty, as we slept safely and soundly in our own room.

What could be more deliciously enjoyable than breakfast outside in this magnificent beauty of mountains and valley! I can see it yet, after thirty years! On the return trek, we stopped at one large Kafir village graveyard. Lifting the lid of the rough wood coffin, we saw the whitened bones of some long dead Kafir, "buried" above ground in the strange manner of this people. Seeing the many coffin boxes stacked under the evergreens, and the curiously carved wooden images leaning against the trees, we felt as if we were in another world in this remote Bumboret valley.

Here dwell in primitive isolation the Kalash people, called Kafirs by the Muslims—meaning infidel or unbeliever. The black-garbed, shell-bedecked women and girls chanted a weird wail as they slowly danced to the beat of the skin drums. Their faces were painted with powdered goats horn and red dye.

Phyllis Irwin, M.D.

We had an eerie feeling of the presence of dark spirits hovering near! Tears filled our eyes and our hearts were stabbed with pain as we realized they are LOST, gripped by Satan, and we knew not one word of their strange tongue to tell them that Christ died for their sins. With the help of a Chitrali translator, and our newly acquired Chitrali vocabulary of 50 or so words, we were able to distribute the remainder of our vitamins and a few other medicines and ointments. They will not use the government dispensary. The men accompanying us were amazed at their enthusiasm for our medicines.

We walked until we were ready to drop; therefore, we chose to go along the stream out of the valley instead of climbing the mountain again. About twenty times we crisscrossed the stream on split logs. Irene was behind me, holding my hand, as she was afraid and dizzy with the swirling water below.

Phyllis Irwin, M.D.

At one point we were so thirsty we gave in to temptation and drank of the stream, to Irene's detriment later. Jack "marched" militarily into Ayun village several minutes behind all of us but with a determined manner! We went back to Chitral city by jeep, which broke down on the way. We were thankful to catch another one, and finally return to our hotel and bed!

Failing Weather Foils Flight

Irene was sick with dysentery all night, but managed to get on the jeep to the airport. The plane however did not arrive from Peshawar. It had turned back before the Lowry Top because of clouds and poor visibility. Soooo, we loaded all our baggage back into the jeep and returned to the hotel for an extra day—perhaps for Irene's benefit! When the next day dawned, we knew the plane would not come, as the sky was all gray with clouds, and there was a cold wind. So back to the reliable, rough, rugged jeep! On the lower slopes the road was muddy from rain, and the driver and his helper had to throw branches and gravel in places for traction. On the higher hairpin curves there was beautiful but dangerous snow. One lumber truck had overturned on one of the curves.

By God's grace we made it over the pass in snow and clouds! At the first stop on the other side the driver had a good wad of cheras (marijuana) to chew and a drink of liquor. The clutch went out, and we coasted sixteen miles to Dir with the driver getting "happier" all the time. We were glad to arrive alive! Our hotel in Dir this time was larger and even had a latrine, but just as filthy as the other one. During the night I felt something on my bed, and turned the flashlight on a big RAT! We pulled the dirty razais (comforters) over our heads and slept anyway!

We were aroused at 3 a.m. to board a bus, bouncing for two hours in pitch darkness over the torturous mountain road. Although it was the first day of the Ramzan fast, one bazaar was cooking tea, so we were all refreshed at dawn. The bus groaned on under the load of the more than ninety passengers inside and on top! We made Peshawar by 1:30 p.m., retrieved our familiar VW and finally headed HOME! We thanked God for the opportunities we had had to share with the very needy Chitral people, not only our medicines, but with many a word of witness and portions of Scripture. God gives the harvest!

Phyllis Irwin, M.D.

19

Fruit

*M*atthew 13:3-8. "A farmer went out to sow his seed. ...some fell along the path, and the birds came and ate it up.....some fell on rocky places....and they withered. Other seeds fell among thorns.... and choked. Still other seed fell on good ground, where it produced a crop."

Those who sow the seed of the Word in Muslim countries find more of the first three types of soil mentioned than the last. Those turning to Jesus are rare, and some who seem to be believers wither, or turn back because of the thorns. But our responsibility as followers of Christ is to sow the Seed "in all nations" and "to all creation." This certainly includes Islamic nations. Our job is to sow, and the Lord will be responsible for the Harvest. But how do you sow in Muslim culture? Many western methods of evangelism will not work in a Muslim culture. In some Muslim countries, even talking about Christ or giving of literature is not only an offense, but against the law. We have been fortunate in Pakistan to have a measure of freedom in "sowing the seed."

SIKANDAR JAN

WHILE THE GOSPEL is not welcome, the presence of a hospital is appreciated by most. We have been able to freely speak of Christ and the Bible in the wards and clinics, and to talk individually to those who are interested. Every morning after a brief chapel service for the Christian staff, the Gospel is presented in a simple way in the out patient clinics and on the wards. Literature is available for those who are literate, and evangelistic staff folks are available to talk with those who are interested. We have found that the women especially, who are so needy and often neglected and abused, are open to a Gospel of love and respond to compassionate care. The first one to believe, as far as we know, was a lady named Sikandar Jan, in 1958. She came in with far advanced breast cancer. She had surgery, which prolonged her life for over a year. While she was with us, she responded to the Gospel and accepted Christ.

MAQBOOL

THE FIRST FRUITFUL contact Russ made was when a man named Maqbool came to church one Sunday when Russ was preaching. He was a teacher in a nearby village. He wanted to talk afterward, and told Russ he had become a Christian twelve years before, but had since turned back to Islam because of the pressures. As they talked, he seemed to be truly repentant and wanted to come back to the Lord.

He came on occasion for months, studying with Russ, attending church services, and often had meals with us. Patty used to call him "Uncle Maqbool." Once he went with another of our missionaries, George McMillan, to a village where he had formerly taught. He gave his testimony to several in the bazaar, until the leading maulvi (religious leader) from the mosque stirred up a couple of hundred school children to hoot them out of town! Some months later Don DeHart and Russ visited him in the rather remote village of Sirikot, where he was teaching. Russ remembers the cock tied to the leg of the bed, which was an effective alarm clock in the wee hours! Later they were served this bird to eat, but he proved very tough! Maqbool had many pressures in the village for being a Christian and finally resigned. He was depressed, wondering what his future would be. Later, his body was found in the Indus River. Whether he had ended his own life, or had it been ended for him we will never know. He was choked out by the thorns of persecution.

SAAJID

SAAJID CAME ALONG years later, a young man who lived right in the village where the hospital is located. His family had a shop in the bazaar. He had first studied the Bible in English with a short term doctor, who referred him to Russ when he left and we returned from furlough. He preferred to speak with Russ in Urdu. He was very afraid his family would learn of his interest, and usually came at night. Sometimes he

Phyllis Irwin, M.D.

crawled over the hospital compound wall so even the gatekeeper would not see him. He seemed to sincerely accept Jesus, and often attended our Sunday night English services. Russ spent hundreds of hours with him over quite a period of time. Then Russ arranged for him to go to Lahore to study for a few weeks at the Theological Education by Extension office. His family got word of this, and sent a cousin to inform him that his mother was very ill and about to die. He came back with him, only to find that his mother was not sick at all. But once home, they threatened him so that he was afraid to pursue his interest further. The seed had been choked out by the thorns.

Over the years, more women began to "cross the line" to belief in the Savior through the hospital ministry. I felt burdened for these new "little sisters" as they had no fellowship, no church family, no one to pray for and disciple them, and usually a hostile family if they made their beliefs known. In addition, most were illiterate. We did follow up as we could, but they were scattered in isolated villages in far-flung places. When they returned to the hospital, our Bible Women would take them aside for teaching, and helped them memorize Bible verses and songs. Visits were made to their homes as feasible. But some lived too far away; some had families who would object.

A monthly fellowship was started for those who could come to clinic on a certain day. They would gather together before or after they had seen the doctor. Once when I was in the USA for furlough, I started what was called "The Little Sister Adoption Program." Prayer partners in churches could "adopt" a group of 3 or 4 converts to pray for, and I would try to send updates from time to time. This continued for 20 years or more, until we retired. We had 25 groups of "little sisters," each prayed for by 4 or 5 ladies. The total count on that adoption list was over 130, over a course of many years. Some were "little brothers" but most were sisters. Of that number, we lost contact with a sizeable number. Some lived too far away for regular return. Some Seed may have fallen on rocky, thorny soil and did not thrive. Some lived close enough for follow up and visits; some came regularly for medicine and fellowship. A number would come to the Christmas celebrations and the monthly fellowships. In many of these lives, it seemed that the Seed had fallen upon good ground. Let me share a few of their stories with you.

THE TWIN SISTERS

SAKINA AND SALIMA were identical twins, married with children. Sakina was brought to the hospital in 1971 on a bed, paralyzed from the neck down. She had difficulty breathing and her color was poor. Obviously, she would not live long in that condition. On examination, we found she had a large TB abscess of her cervical spine. She was put on a spica frame with head traction, to take some of the pressure off, and as soon as possible she had delicate surgery to drain the abscess. She showed immediate improvement in her breathing, and started to move her arms a bit. She was with us for many weeks on TB treatment, and later had the cervical spine fused.

All this time, her twin sister Salima and other relatives were by her side. They heard the Gospel daily, and talked freely with the staff about Jesus. Both the twins and their father put their faith in Christ. Sakina fully recovered. The day they left to go home, the father put on a big "tea" for all the hospital staff. Since they live only ten miles or so away, they were able to come back regularly, and attend the monthly fellowship groups. The father did not dare admit his change of belief in the village, and the twins were not really free in their larger families to practice their faith. We have often visited them and are always welcomed. Sakina lives near Mansehra, but Salima lives a bit farther away on a rugged hilltop with footpath access. They have continued strong in their faith through all these years. We have been able to treat many of this extended family for TB. Salima had pulmonary TB, her son had TB of the kidney, and their mother died of TB. When we returned to Pakistan in 2002, I had a chance to visit the clinic in December. I was delighted to see Sakina, and she was overjoyed to see me! It had been over 30 years since she was brought to us in a dying state!

HUKAM JAN

HUKAM JAN AND Abdul Raoof are from Free Kashmir (meaning the Pakistan controlled area), about 40 miles away, in Muzuffarabad. In the summer of 1978, Hukam Jan was in a government hospital in that city, with a ruptured uterus during labor. However, her tragic condition was not diagnosed, and she lay dying, semi comatose.

She saw a vision of a man in white telling her to go to the mission hospital where she could be saved. When her husband came, she roused enough to be able to tell him of this vision, which they took very seriously. After inquiring where there was a mission hospital, he brought her to us. What a hopeless case! The baby was dead, of course, and she would be soon.

She was taken to surgery, even though there was not much hope. The dead baby was removed, and the uterus repaired. Miraculously, she recovered! As she grew stronger, she told the Bible lady Rehmat about her vision, and asked, "Who was that man in white who told me to come here and be saved?" When she heard it was Jesus, she readily received him as her Savior. Her husband and daughter also believed, and the two little boys as much as they understood. What rejoicing we had when she was able to come to church in a wheelchair and give her testimony before she went home!

Did their neighbors in Kashmir also rejoice? NO! They had heard that they had all become Christians, so they looted their house before they returned! He lost his job, and they received a lot of persecution for their faith. Hukam Jan was so outspoken and eager to witness that she was brought before the police several times. They were both severely beaten. Both are literate; so they could read the Bible. He used to be a teacher in the mosque, which is one reason they were so persecuted. In 1988, ten years after her conversion, she was visiting our evangelist Khurshid, and told her this story: Some zealous Islamic evangelists came to their city, and a lady held a "woman's meeting." When the ladies told her Hukam Jan would not come because she was now a Christian, the lady said, "Then we'll go to her home." There, she railed and ranted against Hukam Jan's faith and against "That Man." Our sister Hukam Jan asked her to leave, upon which they had her arrested. The police had been waiting in front of the house to take her!

At the jail, the warden seeing her said, "What, are you here again? What have you done this time?" She answered, "Nothing. I just believe like I have for 10 years since That Man saved me." She was held and harangued for two days, then finally released. Just a year later, during the monsoon season, the mud roof of their house collapsed in the heavy rains, burying her in the debris. Abdul Raoof and his sons escaped, and the daughter Rukhsana was living elsewhere with her husband. While they grieved their great loss, it was a comfort to know that she is with that Savior she saw in her vision years before!

We visited them for condolence, and they showed us her grave right there in the courtyard. They showed us the rubble of the collapsed house, even as they were working on constructing a new one. Rukhsana told us that no one could take Jesus from her heart, although she cannot live openly as a believer. She has two of the most gorgeous little girls I have ever seen, with big black eyes and outgoing, friendly personalities. I hope she tells them of the Man in white who can save them as he did their Grandmother.

MUSTAFA

MUSTAFA WAS THE mother of two seriously ill young children. She brought them to the hospital accompanied by their grandfather. The children had an incurable blood disorder called thalassemia and were so anemic that they were pale and listless. They were admitted and given blood transfusions to bring their blood count up. For a while, they appeared healthy and energetic, but then as the blood "wore out" they would return for more transfusions. Over many months, blood was given by the missionaries and staff each time they came. Each visit they heard the Gospel, and both always seemed eager to listen and learn more. But they were afraid of anyone in their family knowing of their faith.

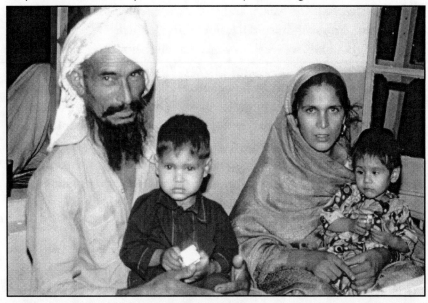

As the children's disease progressed, their spleens enlarged from the old blood, and new blood did not help as much. Gul Nasrin died first. We visited the family in the village shortly before Ali Khan followed his sister into eternity. Our Bible woman Rehmat asked Ali Khan, "Who loves you?" He answered, "Jesus loves me!"

TASLIM

TASLIM WAS AN older, unmarried lady who lived in a nearby town. Her whole family have been very good friends of the hospital. I delivered her nephew, who was born with hypertrophic pyloric stenosis. (This is an obstruction at the end of the stomach, which is fatal if not corrected.) We could not do the surgery at our hospital at that time, but I was able to accompany Taslim and the baby to the city of Lahore to a larger mission hospital where the surgery was successful. I remember visiting the ward the night before surgery, and found Taslim curled up in the crib with the infant!

That baby grew and eventually became a doctor! We have visited the family many times over the years, and eaten many meals and teas with them. Taslim was very faithful to Christ and attended all the monthly fellowship retreats. She often came to the Christmas service at the hospital. Her family never objected, but did not share in her faith. She developed diabetes and was in and out of the hospital for complications. Shortly after one such hospitalization, during which she rejoiced in the Christian fellowship, we received word that our beloved sister had passed away. We went at once to their home, just hours after she had died. The body was lying on a rope bed on the open verandah where we had so often had tea with her. There was a large block of ice at the side of the bed, with a fan blowing over it onto the corpse. There is no embalming, and bodies must be buried within 24 hours. The courtyard and verandah were crowded with ladies who had come to mourn, while the men were in another room. But we did not mourn as those ladies who had no hope, for we knew that Taslim was with the Savior!

ZARINA

ZARINA CAME TO us from Kashmir, a quadriplegic (paralyzed in all four extremities) from a fall. She and her husband were with us for three months while he learned to care for her. He himself had had a back injury and could barely walk with a stick. He was a most unusual Muslim husband, for he truly loved his wife and cared for her so tenderly. The usual treatment of such a handicapped person would be to relegate the care to some woman relative, and before long the patient would die of benign neglect. She never even got a bedsore—remarkable! Hearing the daily ward gospel presentations, and having loving concern shown by ward and evangelistic staff convinced her that God is Love. She put her faith in Jesus, and went home saved even though unhealed! They have five little girls, now cared for by his mother. Hospital staff visited the rude one room house on a hilltop, climbing up a difficult path, and saw how he cared for her.

Zarina showed an unusual openness and interest to hear more about Jesus during this visit, and even stated in clear words that Jesus shed his blood for her sins. They have one cassette in Hindko, the local language, and often listen to it with a neighbor's player. Her husband came monthly for medicines and to report on her condition. He has never made any confession of faith, but is open and friendly. The next winter after her accident, he brought her to the hospital again and asked if they could stay during the cold weather. He was afraid she would die of the cold in their

Phyllis Irwin, M.D.

poorly heated mountain hut. What a bright spot she was in the ward, always smiling and cheerful. Eventually, we lost track of Zarina. She no doubt had gone to be with her Savior.

SAFIA AND RAKHIMA

SAFIA WAS BROUGHT to the hospital after a fall from a tree while cutting leaves for her goats. She also was a paraplegic (paralyzed from the waist down). Her sister Rakhima came to care for her, and was the first to accept Christ, in December 1985, after hearing the gospel message. Rehmat, the Bible woman, brought her down to my house, where I was on bed rest for hepatitis, so that she could give me her testimony. She was very simple, but seemed to understand the basics of the Good News. She was found to have TB, and treatment was started. Safia also accepted Christ, and they went home as believers after some months, with Safia in a wheel chair. In a few weeks they returned, and Safia had brought some carefully embroidered cloth pieces for several of the staff. On one, she had copied the Urdu script of Bible verses even though she can't read! We have been to see her in another sister's remote house up a rocky path on top of a hill in Azad (free) Kashmir. There was no place she could use her wheel chair, so she spent most of her time on a rope bed in a small, dark room. The sister welcomed us, although she is not a believer. Safia was overjoyed, and showed us the sewing and embroidery pieces she does. She has a tape recorder, and listens to Hindko Scripture when "the coast is clear."

We learned that Rakhima is dying of TB, as her husband will not allow her to be treated. When I returned to Pakistan in 1999, two staff members and I were able to go see Safia in another sister's home near Rawalpindi, a large city. This is a much better place, where she has space in a room with much light, and can enjoy visitors. She is still doing hand sewing and seems happy. It was a joy to see her in the faith after so many years!

SHAREEN

SHAREEN IS FROM far away Kohistan (which means "place of the mountains"). She was brought in 1983, with severe complications of childbirth. She had to have surgery, and we despaired of her life. God did raise her up after many weeks of difficulty in healing due to infection. The twin girl survived, but the boy did not. Since her language is completely different, we could not communicate with her except by Kohistani tapes made by Gospel Recordings. Months after her discharge, she returned at Easter and was able to see a filmstrip on the life of Christ, which her brother-in-law translated into Kohistani. She avidly listened, and her outward response indicated that she understood and believed, even though we could not talk with her. Contact has been infrequent, but we know that God understands her situation so much better than we do. Her baby grew to be a healthy little girl. "He who began a good work in you will carry it on to completion until the day of Christ Jesus." (Philippians 1:6.)

KHATIJA

KHATIJA WE HAVE known for many years. She was saved in 1971 at the hospital when her first baby was born. Her husband is a Muslim convert who spent countless hours with my husband Russ studying the Word. He taught Khatija to read so that she could read the Bible. He is very intelligent and educated, but he seems to have a mental problem. He reverted back to Islam several times, back and forth in his faith. He became abusive to Khatija and forbade her to read the Bible. Then he moved the family 80 miles away to the city of Rawalpindi. As he became more unstable and repressive she became stronger in the Lord. When he was more reasonable, visits could be made to her, and they occasionally came for Christmas.

Then, in 1984, Habib suddenly gave her a bill of divorcement and forced her to leave without the children. (Islam allows this.) She pleaded with him to allow her to take the toddler girl of twins, who was small and weak. Her twin brother had to stay with Habib. She fled to her parents, who were not thrilled to have her back, but did allow her to stay. Later she told of sneaking back to the house in hopes of seeing her children while Habib was away. Her oldest son Tahir would not open the door, saying, "We do not want to see you again." She begged him to pull the curtain aside so she could see the younger ones. When they saw her they started crying, and Tahir had tears in his eyes, but fearful of his father, he would not open the door.

Phyllis Irwin, M.D.

She did not see her children for years, but she continued in the faith even though she could not read the Bible in her Muslim family's home. She got a job as a housekeeper/cook in the home of a wealthy family, and her daughter started to school. Hospital staff continued to visit her every two or three months. Habib would visit the Bible Correspondence School office and claim he was a Christian, but was still very unstable. In the spring of 1991, I was able to visit her at her mother's home, with two other staff. She had not seen her other children in seven years. What a surprise it was, then, when on entering the courtyard to visit Khatija, we saw her oldest son, Tahir! I hardly recognized him, as he was now a grown man.

At that time he was actually living with his mother, as he had defied his father and visited her. When Habib found out, he kicked him out of his house, and forbade him ever to come back to see his siblings. He had brought his little brother, the other twin, the first time he visited his mother. When the little boy was told she was his mother, he said, "She cannot be my mother. My mother is dead." What a heartbreak for Khatija, but at least she got to see him once. Tahir then lived with his mother, and did well in college. He tutored other students to earn money.

The last time I saw Khatija was in 1999. We found her in another relative's home, with ALL of her children except one girl! One by one, they had all "escaped" from Habib and chose to live with their mother. The one girl who stayed with Habib had been denied an education by her father, so that she would be able to do the work in the home. Tahir is now a doctor! The next girl is an R.N. with a very good job at one of the leading hospitals in the city. The twins, now united, are both doing well in school. The boy twin had not been allowed to go to school (reflecting Habib's twisted mind) so that when he came to his mother, he had to start in first grade, even though he was a big boy. He progressed rapidly, and is now almost up with his twin sister! We had a time of worship with all of this united family, and gave praise to God who had worked a real miracle! Habib still occasionally visits the Bible Correspondence School office, wearing a long white robe and now claims that he is both a Christian and a Muslim!

BIBI JAN

BIBI JAN IS a Gujar lady (a nomadic goat herding people) who had bowel resection surgery in 1979 due to TB. We were surprised one day after morning ward devotions to hear her declare in front of all the people in the ward, "That is right what your Book teaches. Jesus is the Son of God and the Savior." Her husband listened in the men's ward, and although he made no commitment, neither did he seem to object to her faith. She is illiterate, but her son reads and has Gospel portions.

They continued to come to the hospital when they weren't traveling with their herds. Often they would bring other patients to be seen. She was there with her sick adult daughter over Christmas one year and enjoyed the fellowship and activities very much. Her son, Ghulam Mustafa, seemed to have crossed the line! He would often read to his mother, and they listened to a small hand wound tape recorder and scripture cassettes loaned to them by the hospital fellowship group.

In 1984 she and her son came in the fall after bringing their herds back down from the high Kaghan Valley, with a sad story that the tape recorder, a valuable horse, and some clothes had been stolen during the summer. They came on a retreat day, when the believers meet for fellowship. They were not seeking material help, but the comfort and sympathy of their Christian "family".

In later years, Bibi Jan developed serious health problems. She was admitted in 1990 very sick with asthma, diabetes and related complications. She did hear the Word each morning in the ward before rounds, and was visited at the bedside by the evangelists. This is where we have to leave her, close to the time when she would be gathered to her Savior.

SALAH-U-DIN

SALAH-U-DIN WAS A schoolboy living far north in Hunza, not far from China. His father had a government job as a toll collector on the Karakorum highway, collecting from Chinese truck drivers bringing goods into Pakistan. Salah-u-Din would often warm himself by the wood fire his mother cooked on when he came home from school, as it is cold in the high mountains. One day as he squatted too close to the fire, his clothes caught on fire. He panicked and ran. He had never been taught, "Stop, Drop, and Roll." He was severely burned. No medical help was available, so he just lay on a rope bed in terrible agony for several days. His family was distraught, but had no recourse.

One day when the boy was near death, a man came to the toll stop who knew Muhubat Shah, the father. When he heard his story, he said, "Why don't you take him to Qalandarabad near Mansehra, where there is a mission hospital?" Muhubat Shah had never heard of the hospital, which was two days travel away. No one from his area had ever gone that far for treatment. It must have taken a great deal of faith in this faint hope to make the decision to take his son that far. They told the mother and sisters good-bye, not knowing whether or when they would be back. The boy lay for many hours on the back seat of a bus jolting over the narrow highway etched onto the side of the mountains of the Karakorum Range of the Himalayas.

When they arrived at Bach Christian Hospital, the boy was an almost hopeless case, with third degree burns over much of his body, severely dehydrated, anemic, infected, and malnourished. He was given intravenous fluids and blood donated by staff. As the infection was treated, he was encouraged to eat and gain strength. After many days he was strong enough for the first of several skin graft operations to cover his wounds. It took several months, but he slowly healed. Daily he and his father listened to the Word presented in the ward, and talked with the Christian staff. Both accepted the Lord and began to study correspondence courses on the Bible. By the time they left, they were well grounded in their faith. It was a great day when we saw them off on the bus to Hunza!

Weeks later we heard of their homecoming. The villagers had told Salah-u-Din's mother that he surely must be dead, and that Muhubat Shah was probably not going to come back. But when they got off the bus that day, some thought the healthy little boy must be a ghost! However, he was real. His mother and sisters were overjoyed! They were eager to tell them of their long adventure, their new faith, and of the One who had really healed Salah. The whole family quickly became believers. The townspeople were so impressed that they also listened, and did not object to their new faith. That whole Muslim area is much more tolerant than elsewhere in Pakistan; so they had no persecution.

Muhubat would go with some of our visiting Christians in the summer to distribute tracts in the bazaar. When he was put on night duty at the toll booth, he said he did not need to have anyone with him. Two men were usually put on night duty, as they are afraid of the ghosts that walk at night. Muhubat said he had someone with him constantly who protected him. What a testimony! That family is the only Christian presence in the whole district of Hunza.

A couple of years later at Easter time, the whole family came to celebrate with their Christian family at the hospital. The mother and sisters had never been out of their mountains before. They came to the monthly retreat, although they could understand nothing of the words. They speak only Sheena, while the males know Urdu, the national language taught in schools. But they understood the love demonstrated.

On Easter morning, after the service in our chapel, they were baptized at the hospital in a wading pool. What a joyous demonstration of Resurrection! Years later after retirement, when I had returned to work for a few weeks, I was called out of women's clinic one day by the evangelist. Salah-u-Din had come and wanted to see me. He was a grown young man with a job in nearby Mansehra! What a thrill to see him looking so well and to know he is still a faithful believer! This family is part of the good fruit.

Nazir Ahmad

In Azad Kashmir (the part controlled by Pakistan), where missionaries are no longer allowed to work, a small number of converts from the hospital ministry developed. A teacher, Nazir Ahmed, and his wife believed, and came to some of the monthly fellowship week-ends. It is encouraging that the wife also came to the Lord, for a divided household causes difficulties.

Hussan Shah

Another man, Hussan Shah, first came to the hospital as an outpatient, but went away in disgust without registering to be seen. This was because he saw the scripture verse in the out patients' waiting area, "Jesus Christ came into the world to save sinners." He wanted nothing to do with Christianity. But after he had a vision, in which he was told to go back and find out what that verse meant, he came for instruction and soon was eager to study the Word. Since then, as foreigners cannot enter that area, some of our Pakistani staff has visited him in Kashmir.

He has not been to any of the fellowship meetings, perhaps because of unknown persecutions and pressures by family.

ZUBEDA

RECENTLY SOME OF our Pakistani women staff were visiting hospital contacts in Kashmir when they were called into a house as they were passing by. A lady named Zubeda told them she recognized their voices as being from the hospital, and wanted to see them. She said she had heard about Jesus during several outpatient visits and wanted to hear more. They had a good opportunity with her, and she told them she truly believed. Others of the household were angry and told her since they knew of her interest and reasons for wanting to go to the hospital; there would be no more visits for her. She replied, "Even if you put me out of the house, I will still have the Lord with me."

SULTAN

ONE MORNING IN our chapel staff devotions before rounds, a young man with a beard, wrapped in a blanket, stood up and said, "I used to be a Muslim." We listened eagerly to his testimony, as we had followed his spiritual progress for some time with prayer and interest. He had come initially while still a student for the Muslim priesthood, to study the Bible of the Christians. He admitted that at first his motives had been far from pure, but as he read and studied, the Holy Spirit did a work in his heart through the Word. After much hesitation and consideration, he made his decision for Christ.

His family was incensed, and attempted to bring him back to the Muslim faith by beating him and burning his Bible before him. The night his brother had planned to take his life, an older sister warned him and helped him to escape. He went off to Bible School, but had not been there very long before his father and brother came and forcibly took him away. Nothing was heard of him for a long time, and we were much in prayer for his safety. On a certain day simultaneous prayer meetings were organized to be held at the Bible School and at each of our stations to intercede for him. Just hours before the prayer meetings, Sultan himself walked into our Bookroom in Abbottabad! Russ and the nationals who were there at the time said it seemed almost like Peter returning from prison! He told us that morning in chapel that his father had taken him far into Azad Kashmir and left him with an uncle to work as a forester. He told his son that this was the last time he was going to "help" him, and that if he left the uncle's care, it would be as if he had left the family and would no longer be considered a part of them. Sultan worked about a week, and then decided to run away and return to civilization. As he wandered back, he would cut grass or corn with the villagers he met, and eat with them. Several times he gave them his testimony in the evenings when the work was done, until they would become angry and call him a "kafir" (heretic). Yet he rejoiced in the opportunity to witness. That evening the scheduled prayer meetings for him turned into praise meetings!

These dear Little Sisters and Brothers are typical of the "crop." Add to these a few score more, including Sisters Roshan Jan, Pari Jan, and Brother Niamatullah described in the chapter on Lowly People. This is certainly not a picture of a thriving church by our standards. It is scattered in the mountains and villages of the Northwest Frontier, and the believers are unable to meet together or even practice their faith openly in their own homes. But they are beloved of God, chosen in Him before the foundation of the world, and precious in his sight.

20

F.C. College Lahore

FIRST IMPRESSIONS OF LIVING IN A BIG CITY

To get to 8 FCC one must face the Lahore traffic. It is not so alarming at 5 AM, but during rush hours, or anytime during the day and evening, it is a chaotic tangle of cars, busses, trucks, vans, motorcycles, bicycles, horse carts and pedestrians. Vehicles move 3 or 4 abreast in two lanes, vying for position, weaving in and out with inches to spare, leaving a newcomer amazed that there are not more "fender benders" than there are. All this is with much honking of horns and lack of observance of traffic rules. Once in a traffic jam when cars were at a stand still, Russ was abreast of a Suzuki van driver who was furiously honking. Russ good naturedly told him that his horn wouldn't help traffic move. His jovial reply, "I know, but I just enjoy honking!"

PLUMBING: In my estimation, this is about as badly done in this country as obstetrics (and that is pretty bad!). It is best to approach the situation with humor. For instance, when I first flushed the toilet at 8 FCC shortly after arrival, I was surprised to find that about half the water gushed across the floor instead of going into the commode! Luckily, it went into a drain conveniently placed near the tub. The flush is a tank near the ceiling, so one pulls a chain to release the water. As the tank refills, it also leaks and dribbles down the pipe in the corner, furnishing a constant trickle to the same drain. The only way to stop this annoying trickle is to reach high up on the pipe and turn off the valve. Not very convenient!

While we are in the bathroom, I'll mention the tub, which is made of concrete and polished chips (like terrazzo floors). The polished surface still does not compare with a smooth enameled tub! However, I am thankful for a tub. But while workmen were putting up white tile in back of the sink and tub, they slopped cement all over the tub, and into the drain. This gave us a lot of exercise chipping off the cement with a screw driver and scrubbing it down with a wire brush. Thank goodness for a handyman husband! He cleared the drain of all the rubble. Now to the kitchen: I was not too surprised when the sink faucet did not work. It required one to bend over and turn on the valve under the sink every time water was needed! Then when the water drained from the sink, it also left a trail across the floors. Another interesting feature, which is not easily repairable, is air in the lines. This is an unremitting condition in many old houses here. So when a faucet is turned on, there is great spitting and hissing as water and air gush out together. Sometimes this is with force enough to give one an unexpected shower! There must be many leaks in the old water lines where air can enter.

STOVE: This appliance is a two burner gas stove which sits on the counter top. Without an oven, all my new baking utensils will be useless, and we will be without cookies and other necessities. It was coated with years of grease and grime accumulation that had to be scraped off with chisel and screw driver before soap and water could be applied. Its unique feature is the way it is lighted. To light the burners, one has to reach arm's length under the burner to turn on the shut off valve. If one forgets to turn off this valve after cooking, soon the smell of gas permeates the kitchen and alerts one to do the needful. Still we are thankful for piped in gas here in Lahore, which is cheap and plentiful. We don't have to depend on the irregular supply of cylinders as we did at Bach Hospital. After discovering all its peculiarities, we decided to replace the counter top stove with a real stove.

FLOORS: These are of concrete, pitted and cracked so that the "seams" are up to an inch wide. This adds to the challenge of cleaning, as the hand brush does not thoroughly clean crevices. In one particularly wide crack in the kitchen I found the remains of a small metal pin which said, "Smile, God loves you!" I thought that very appropriate! Hope for the floors include a mason to fill up the cracks while we are gone to annual conference. We can then put our old rugs down. These were spared from the fire, which destroyed most of our possessions in the storage building where we had stored them during furlough. Fortunately, the Condies had been using the rugs.

CREATURES: We share the house with an assortment of lizards, ants, cockroaches, scorpions, and furry creatures called shrews. No doubt there are mice, too, which have not yet put in an appearance. Food left on a counter for even a few minutes will be found by the ants. War has been made on them with a lethal powder sprinkled in cabinets and around edges of counters. Each morning the night's toll must be brushed off the counters. A new rat trap finished off a shrew just a few minutes after setting it. One creature that we welcome is the ubiquitous lizard. This small gecko lives on the screens and ceilings. It is very useful as its diet is flies, mosquitoes and moths. It is fun to watch them on a screen at night as they stalk their prey. It is fascinating to watch them catch a moth by its head (never by the other end) and slowly swallow. The fluttering of wings gradually ceases, and the moth is gone! Outside in the trees we often see the colorful parrots and hear their chatter. Not so melodic are the huge flocks of crows, which gather in the trees by the hundreds for their evening raucous concert.

NOISES: Having never lived in a big city in Pakistan, we had to get used to the background hum of city noise and traffic. An abundance of old trees softens the noise. Our being on a large campus also blunts it. There are 7000 male resident students. Many of the 250 teachers are also housed on campus. But the background noise is often pierced by the gunshots celebrating weddings or who know what, the shrill of sirens or beating of drums. Daily at 4:30 a.m. there develops a cacophony of the first call to prayer from the loudspeakers of scores of mosques all over the city. They are not synchronous, but begin with a few, building to a crescendo and then tapering off in about half an hour. Some mosques decide to preach or intone long passages of the Quran, so the noise continues for about an hour.

FIRE BLACKENED SALVAGE: One of the few things not destroyed in the storage room fire that destroyed most of our belongings was our silverware set. I spent several hours on this, which was intact in a charred box, although every piece was greatly blackened. Using a strong silver dip cleaner, plus lots of elbow grease, most of the pieces came out clean, even though a bit dulled from all the scrubbing. After a few hours my hands turned a dirty brown as if they had been painted with silver nitrate! This took several days to wear off. I spent many hours rubbing and scrubbing on the remains of the china set we salvaged from the fire. The gold pattern came off some pieces which needed vigorous scrubbing with rough pads and cleanser, but we do have some usable pieces. One can tell they have been literally "through the fire."

Next, attention was turned to the pans, lids, and trays we salvaged. Some had plastic welded onto them along with the black. Our new house helper Khurshid proved to be a good worker. She worked for hours with a stone, wire brush, metal pot scrubber, and cleanser. When she finished with a piece, I would work hours more, with VIM (a local brand of cleanser) and VIGOR (my own), plus putty knife, scrubber and metal pad. My right hand suffered many small punctures from the steel wool, and the sweat rolled. But at long last I have clean and shining pots! Some handles need to be replaced with wooden ones. We haven't even begun on the scorched linens we salvaged. Some only have minor damage, but smell very much of fire and ash. This will require at least two washings in the small machine that Marty used last term. It will do two sheets or the equivalent in each load, and the hot water must be poured in from the sink by filling a big pan. Thankfully, we have a water heater, which heats moderately well.

MISCELLANEOUS: The kitchen, bedroom, and other cabinets were all missing at least half their handles. One door had to be pried open with a knife; a nail served as the knob on a drawer until Russ replaced them with the real thing. These old metal window frames have permanent screen and iron bars on the outside for security purposes; so they cannot swing open to the outside. To open a window, the whole thing is drawn inside the room by an attached metal bar. All the small panes were smeared with paint left by careless workmen, and required a razor blade to get them clean. The bathroom windows were particularly hard, as they were not only "decorated" with dried paint, but covered with paper glued on the inside for a curtain effect. When I had them clean, I covered the outside of the panes with opaque plastic for privacy. One of the several good features of the house is storage shelves in the bedrooms. They are concrete, five shelves floor to ceiling, with wooden doors. It just took several hours to scrub them down and chase out the spiders before we could use them. The shelves served as dresser drawers. I found flat plastic baskets help organize our socks, underwear, etc. There is also a small walk-in hanging closet in each bedroom. One can tell the houses were built for missionaries long ago, for the usual Pakistani houses have little or no storage space.

YARD: This is one thing I appreciate just the way it is! There is a spacious yard all around the house, screened off from the campus street on two sides, and high hedges and tall shade trees of the neighbors on the other two. Three sides have grass, flowers and shrubs, which are kept in good condition by a part time gardener who comes every evening for a couple of hours to water, sweep leaves, and transplant. The fourth side in back of the house has a place for hanging clothes, room for a vegetable garden, where I can plant lettuce, snow peas and a few other things. Seasons are the same as in USA but because this is semi-tropical, fall is the planting season, and flowers bloom best in February and March. We have a lime tree which is bearing fruit, and a couple of frangipani trees. I always wondered what that word meant in the old IU school song! Ivy and other vines cover some of the outside windows for coolness, and the front verandah hosts about 50 potted plants of many varieties.

WEATHER: Upon our arrival the last of September, temps were in the 90's and it was very dry and dusty. Fans were going day and night, and two showers a day seemed necessary to feel presentable. They said it had cooled off, that it had been up to 115-120 most of the summer. It was so hot that all the mosquitoes and flies had died off. So there is some compensation to the hot weather! Now the mosquitoes are making a comeback, and the flies will be happy all winter on the garbage heaps which are found here and there on the street corners. Now, in mid-October, the weather has really turned pleasant, with 80's in the day and cool nights and mornings.

EDITORIAL NOTE: OUR last term we moved to Lahore to be near Russ's ministry with Theological Education by Extension, later known as Open Theological Seminary. He had helped found this ministry and had made many trips to Lahore over the years. Forman Christian College had been taken over by the government a number of years before and was now a Muslim school. We were allowed to live in an old missionary residence on the campus. The other side of the house held the TEE office.

21

The Punjabi Church

LAHORE 1993

*W*e decided to drive to church one Sunday morning, since we were short on time. Once in the car, we realized that at 8:20 a.m. the morning "rush" of traffic is at a peak. It took us thirty minutes to get there by car, whereas we could have made it in 15-20 minutes on foot! We parked the car on a side road and walked back a narrow bricked alleyway teeming with activity. Dirty children were playing; pedestrians were avoiding the open drainage coming from the walled courtyards; and sometimes a motorcycle would squeeze by. A high wall encloses the Bethany Church compound. Like an oasis, green trees in the courtyard added some coolness to the warm morning.

Leaving our shoes out on the verandah, we stepped into the big, airy, well-lit worship room which is devoid of furniture except for a few benches along the back wall for those who cannot sit on the floor. There is a pulpit at the front and a small table that holds the communion service. Russ joined the men on their side, and I went to the women's side, sitting cross-legged on the colorful thin cotton rug that had been spread over the concrete floor. Singing has been in progress for some time. People come at all times during the service; so our being late was only cultural.

The atmosphere was quiet and respectful, even though there was continual coming and going of the children, or someone going for a drink from the cooler outside, where they use a communal cup. Outside courtyard walls hawkers yelled loudly of their wares. The young man leading the service called for prayer, whereupon spontaneous prayers continued until he called for another song. We sang in Punjabi, to the

Phyllis Irwin, M.D.

accompaniment of a baja, a small keyboard with bellows. With the left hand the musician operates the bellows; with the right, he plays the tune on a small keyboard. There is no time constraint, and the people sing and pray with real enjoyment and enthusiasm. After half an hour or so, two elders went up and served communion, with more prayers and songs of thanksgiving. The bread was a chapati (flat unleavened bread) from which each participant broke off a small piece. The wine was diluted raisin juice, served from a common glass, one for the men and one for the women. As a modest nod to hygiene, the lip of the glass was wiped with a tissue between participants. The next part of the worship was the offering. During singing, everybody got up (by now I was stiff and had a bit of trouble "unfolding" to stand up!) and filed by a box on the small table placed in the center of the room. After depositing the offerings in the box, we got back into our rows on the floor. I tried a new position!

The pastor made announcements, acknowledged visitors, gave prayer requests, and asked two new couples who had just been married during the past week to come forward. The bashful brides in new fancy outfits and jewelry stepped up beside their husbands. One young man was in the usual shalwar qamais, but the other was outfitted in suit and tie. There was a prayer of dedication, with an elder and the pastor laying hands on the couples.

By now there were about 100 people in the worship room. After more singing, an hour and a half into the service, the speaker is introduced. Padre Hidayat presented none other than Russell Irwin, who is known to the congregation from previous visits to Lahore. Russ had come somewhat prepared, for he knew that any time he appeared at this church, he might be asked to speak. No previous arrangement or preparation is deemed necessary! So, barefoot and wearing shalwar qamais, he preached in excellent Urdu (his first sermon of this term!) from Romans 10. He involved the audience in his teaching, asking for responses periodically, which kept people interested and awake. Most were awake anyway, as sitting cross-legged on a hard floor keeps one from dozing.

After the service there was much greeting among the respective sexes only—not much mixing. The pastor did greet me and gave a hearty welcome. He and his wife have both taken many TEE classes and are well acquainted with the program and with Russ. Some friendly young girls asked me many questions. I also talked with the only other missionary couple there—German Brethren folks we have known for many years. I had done a Caesarian Section on the wife twenty or so years ago. In this Brethren church we truly felt the Lord was glorified and these people had a joyful worship experience. We were welcomed as one of them.

22

Pakistan Revisited

Nov '98-Jan '99

Three and a half years after we officially retired from the work in Pakistan, we were back in Pakistan for a visit! The years of absence soon melted away as we searched for the six Irwin faces in the swirling crowds at the airport. They whisked us away to the safety of home, through the familiar yet daunting, chaotic traffic that observes no rules and has little regard for safety. Thus began our ten-week visit with Nate & family and Cindy in Rawalpindi/Islamabad. It also included ministry in our hospital at Qalandarabad plus visits in Lahore.

It was great being with the kids and grandkids and share with them in the Thanksgiving and Christmas holidays. Marty was successfully home schooling Tim, Jessica, and Leslie. They seemed happy in their spacious, beautiful home in Rawalpindi. It was a joy to see our family "in ministry" and to join their activities.

A short synopsis by statistics is that we made 95 visits in 81 different places, including 8 village visits. We visited Pakistanis, Afghans, Little Sisters (believers from our hospital ministry), numerous Afghan believers including ten Afghan ladies Cindy works with, and some family groups. We attended two Christmas programs put on by Afghan worship groups (unbelievable just a few years ago!) plus the ESL Christmas program put on by Cindy, staff and students. I worked at Bach Christian Hospital two different weeks seeing patients. I did visitation with our young Pakistani lady evangelist in the late afternoons and spoke at Little Sisters Retreat, Nurses Christian Fellowship, and at ward devotions. Russ preached in at least four churches and at several functions. He taught several days at Zarephath Bible Institute, and we both taught English as Second Language classes at Cindy's school. A First Aid class for four different groups was received with interest and enthusiasm.

We were able to see Safedie just a few days before she died. We had asked the Lord to keep her alive until we could see her, which we did the day after we arrived. She had taken care of all three kids when they were young, and worked in our home for almost thirty years. It was a poignant visit. She has been very dear to our family. Her son Rekhan had told us she knew we were coming and seemed to cling to life until we were there. A few days later when we were there again, she was semi- comatose and unable to communicate. She died that night.

The whole time was very rewarding and fulfilling. We saw our hospital well run and progressing in every department under mostly Pakistani direction. We were gratified to see the evangelistic outreach and spiritual tone still sharp and effective. Staff members were most gracious to us, inviting us to teas, suppers, and even breakfasts! We rejoice that some of the staff children, now grown up, have returned to minister. One family has two daughters now teaching at our mission school in nearby Abbottabad; a son is graduating from Medical School and will be on our doctor staff! A niece of a long-term staff member is already on staff as a lady doctor. Dr. Abana's mother reminded us that I delivered her, but neither of us remembers the event! For the first time in BCH's history, there are enough RN's, and they all are Pakistani! The highlight was a staff Awards Program, at which we showed a set of old slides showing the hospital and staff from 1956 to 1990. The staff greatly appreciated seeing their facilities in light of what they had been for several years as the hospital was developing.!

The Zarephath Bible Institute facilities at our TEAM headquarters building are surprisingly nice, considering what the old building was like before renovation. The evening school was encouraging and well attended even though tuition is charged! Nate was tracking down two more possible land sites for the new campus, with a real possibility that one or the other would actually go through. He and the family greatly enjoy living separate from the school compound. When he is at home, he is really at home, not still on campus as he was in Attock. There he was "on call" 24 hours a day. That makes for better family life and freshness in the school situation.

Phyllis Irwin, M.D.

A week in Lahore went quickly as we visited friends. Russ preached several times. The new Theological Education by Extension office building is a vast improvement on the quarters we shared with the office our last term. There is plenty of room for offices, library, meeting rooms and more. The number of TEE teaching centers is increasing in various parts of the country. We attended the staff Christmas lunch and visited in several of their homes. Russ took the revised Eschatology course he had finished and spent some time with staff on it. Cindy was with us the first five days—her first "getaway" in months and we enjoyed some times shopping, and even went to the newest sensation—McDonalds! We stayed with a devout Muslim family who are good friends. Not enough time to do and see all we wanted!

Back in Islamabad, it was a joy to see Cindy in action! She teaches in the afternoons. When at home, either the phone is ringing or someone is at the front door. She is meeting and discipling six different families or groups, some regularly and some occasionally. Others pop up with requests to find out more about Jesus, and want time with her. What a thrill for us to have a long visit with Megan and her younger brother Tariq in Cindy's home. Her faith is strong although she is closely monitored by relatives and can't get out regularly for fellowship.

We were so glad to be in the Azar's home, which is a one-room walkup without furniture. They share a kitchen and tiny bath with another family. Their three boys are adorable, almost like triplets although they are a year or so apart. We were with numerous Afghans, either in their homes or at Cindy's. On at least two occasions she was able to clearly present the Gospel for the first time to some who had never heard. To observe their rapt attention with eyes intent on her face as she told them of Jesus the Savior was worth the trip in itself! As Cindy said later, "That's why we are here!" We heard many agonizing refugee stories, told calmly in the course of conversations, but we wonder what deep emotional scars there are. Only Jesus can heal.

We observed an increasing political unrest. The economy is on the brink with a noticeable increase in population resulting in pollution and overcrowding everywhere. On public transport, passengers perch on top of busses and vans, hang on the back and out of the doors. Then there is the grossly inadequate sanitation, lack of clean water, and very crowded housing which make our slums look like the suburbs. There have been riots in various places over the lack of the staple whole-wheat flour, and cutting hours of electricity due to power shortages. The Army has been called out to control sectarian fighting in Karachi, and to run the government agency for power and water, even though it is failing because of corruption.

Corruption is rampant in every area of society. There is religious unrest, with Sunnis frequently bombing Shia mosques and shooting men at their prayers. Persecution of Christians is not infrequent. Anti-Christian and anti-west feelings fluctuate with current events. Yet we are not discouraged, as our omnipotent sovereign God is still in charge of the world! The time is one of strategic opportunity for the Gospel, and we sense our Pakistani and Afghan Christians are increasingly aware of their responsibility of sharing the Good News. We are so glad our children can be part of the picture, and that we have had the chance to share a bit of what is going on in their lives and ministry.

We had good health the whole time, and the Urdu, Hindko and Pushto came back for use as necessary! It was in every way a successful trip, including the week we spent visiting missionary colleagues and relatives in London, Yorkshire, and Scotland on the way out. A dream fulfilled! All praise to our Lord who made it possible.

Phyllis Irwin, M.D.

23

Visiting Pakistan - Again

APRIL 9, 1999

This time I was traveling alone. It was a very loong journey. In Chicago I was told the BA flight to London was cancelled! 2 options: leave at once on another flight, without luggage. "Oh, but they will deliver it to you the next day!"—like fun they would! Little do they know! Or, go on Air India leaving about 30 minutes later than the original BA one. Let's go for that. OK, but you will have to reclaim your checked bags and take them to the Air India counter. (Sigh. Wait an hour or so.)

When the bags did come, the one with the school books had burst open at one corner, exposing books and an endotracheal tube! I took the yellow strap and put it long ways around to help hold. The BA lady then got a big heavy plastic bag and we wrestled the whole suitcase into it. By then 3 nearby men travelers took pity on two ladies and pitched in. The suitcase was re-strapped on the outside of the plastic, re-roped, and re-inforced with some wide plastic tape. Still looked fragile, but I trundled it down to Air India and prayed it would get through intact. It did!

On the London flight I sat by a nice young man who was a British rock musician, so we talked about bands and "ska" (he knew what that is!), and about my grandson Nathan being in a ska band. I ate rice, curry, and yogurt and slept some. We landed way out in the boonies at Heathrow and were bussed at least 10 miles through the guts of Heathrow to "Arrivals," where the door was not automatic! Another mile or two walk through corridors, up escalators, down halls, to another bus which then went another ten miles to terminal 4. By now my carry-on was getting heavy (no carts). More walking finally got me to a BA check-in counter for all flights. As I was at the desk, someone tapped my shoulder. "You must be Phyllis Irwin!" It was Dr. Dave Beatty, who had just gotten in! He was on his way to work at Bach Hospital. We got a cart and found a place to sit in the big gate area with lots of shops. He was easy to get acquainted with, quite a talker and outgoing; so the hours passed quickly. He was 54, well acquainted with our fellow missionaries the Blanchards, Mitchells, and Eunice. He was head of surgery at U. of Toronto and was in transition to Pakistan for two months. His wife is a PhD in molecular biology and will be coming to join him in May. They have three grown sons. We got seats together on the flight and continued our chat. I told him much about Bach, Islam, etc.

We arrived on time—quite warm but still comfortable even in the arrival hall. Once outside, the crowds were denser than ever, as a Haj pilgrimage flight had just arrived with all the returning pilgrims from Mecca. Hundreds of relatives met them showering them with rose petals. Dave Mitchell, who took Dr.Beatty in tow, had to park out on the street, and Nate was at the far end of the parking lot. It was SO good to see the five Irwins! Tim is taller than ever, and the girls have grown, too. We came home to another breakfast with huge red strawberries, which are in abundance now. Fun unpacking suitcases. The girls were so excited over their Calvert school books, and the males loved the basketball clippings. Cindy called later, after the Easter program. She said it went well, and Rachel (ESL student interested in Christianity) was there. I'll see Cindy tomorrow.

April 23, 1999

I HAD A good week-end with Nate and family, as well as Cindy, before coming north to the hospital. After the first week of work here, I was able to go back to Islamabad for another weekend. On Saturday Tim involved me in a Monopoly game five minutes after I got in the door! The weekend passed all too soon, and I returned to Bach Hospital.

I was soon immersed in the hospital work. There could hardly be a more pleasant place to stay and work, as spring at Bach is lovely! The fragrance of blooming drake and citrus trees perfumes the air, and the bold reds of the bottle brush and flame of the forest trees splash across the landscape. Flowers in profusion unfold their beauty - amaryllis, larkspur, geraniums, daisies, sweet peas, honeysuckle and roses of all hues. I have a large peace rose in my front garden which is almost heartbreaking in its beauty. I have had a dark red long stem bud on my table for almost a week as it slowly opens.

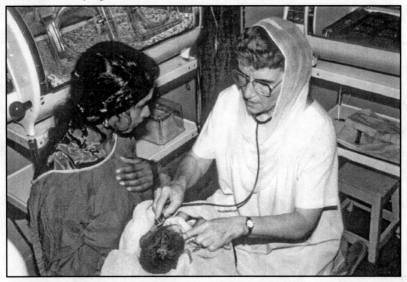

My days started at 5 a.m.. I put on the Pakistani version of running clothes and fast walked for half an hour on my old route around the apple orchard and surgery building. I walked or jogged this for many years, so memories are stirred as I stepped out the door into the cool of the morning to the pervading fragrance of the trees and the haunting call of the ever present cuckoo bird in the distance. Other birds occasionally made their appearance—the tree pie with its long forked tail, the elusive bird of paradise with its beautiful, graceful swishing white tail, the parrots, mynahs, crows in abundance, and even a Himalayan Robin Royale appeared one day. After breakfast (the only meal I seem to be able to eat at home, as I have been invited out so often in the evenings) and devotions, it was off to the ward for rounds at 7 a.m.. Chapel was at 7:45 a.m. with the full staff, who then scatter to duty or to preach in the wards and clinics.

We doctors have a short, informal staff meeting after chapel, and then are off to clinic. Some doctors may be operating, while others see clinic patients. We have more staff than ever I had the privilege of working with when I was here full time. Although the majority of clinic patients are routine and repetitive, there are some very interesting patients who present real challenges in therapy. There are lots of diabetics, hypertensives, many infertility patients, TB, and kids with pneumonia. Lots of obstetric patients, some of which are quite complicated. Today there were three emergency C. Sections in addition to a regular surgery schedule. At noon I had lunch with single and visiting staff in the "mess." We go back to the patients until the 250 or so who were given numbers early in the morning, are seen. We finished at 4 or 4:30 p.m..

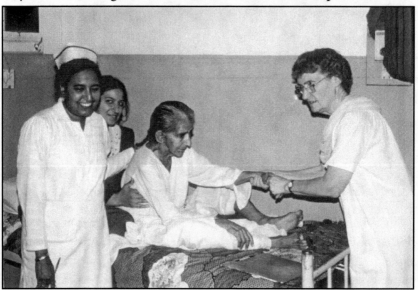

Today there were eighty who had been waiting all night in the gate area to obtain numbers, but they still had to turn away several scores of "late comers" who arrived at 8 a.m. or after and were told the numbers were gone. Some wait two or three days, some try several times to get numbers before they succeed. If they really need to be seen monthly or weekly, we flag their charts so they get a number. After clinic is done, I usually have a tea invitation to some former patient's home or to a staff home here on the compound. Some days I just get back from tea and have to go to a supper invite!

I have seen many old friends and patients who recognize me in the clinic; so we have big hugs and greetings. Pari Jan was here the second day I worked, bringing a surgical patient from her village. She followed me to the dining room and had a big plate of food in the kitchen while the doctors and nurses ate. She was so thankful her patient with a huge ovarian cyst had successful surgery.

We have two surgeons operating most days all day long; and still the list goes on. I am so happy at the spiritual emphasis that has been carried on, with active witnessing and visitation. Besides chapel, the staff has regular prayer meetings, a prayer chain once a month for 24 hours, a nurse's fellowship, Sunday services, women's meetings and more. There are fewer expatriate personnel than when I worked at Bach. All but one of the leadership positions are now filled by responsible Pakistani Christians. They are doing a great job. A class of nurse aides is being trained, a lab student is being upgraded in training, and a lady evangelist-in-training is doing well. It is so gratifying to see how the Lord has worked and is working in many lives. It was a thrill to be able to be a part of it again—at least for a short while!

24

A Woman Travels Alone

May 29, 1999 A Trip to Islamabad

*A*t the crowded, noisy bus stand in Abbottabad, the area for vans to Islamabad is easily found near the main road. I approach the first one in line and pay for 2 tickets for the front seat up by the driver. Not my choice, as there one can see all the chaotic driving head-on, but for a lone, white woman there is no other option. A Pakistani woman would never travel alone, and to sit in the regular seats requires having a male companion. The van is stationary until filled to capacity with passengers. A hawker stands outside, calling to the passing crowds, "Islamabad, Islamabad, leaving now!" Slowly the passengers fill the bus. They are mostly men, but a few heavily veiled ladies in burkas accompanied by men also climb on. I drape my doputta scarf more securely on my head. It is hot. I roll down the window, but that only invites the beggars to approach, pleading with open hand for a few rupees. Vendors also come by, offering strips of coconut, raisins, peanuts, and candies. I roll the window back up.

When the van is packed with its human cargo, we take off and I grab the "panic bar" as we careen down the curvy mountain road to Havelian. It is a relief to get to the level plain and relax a bit. We pass group after group of Gujar folk walking north with their flocks of sheep and goats, to the high mountain pastures. They are a lowly minority people of migrant herdsmen. What a hard life! Walking all day with the animals, camping at night in fields along the roadside, traveling for weeks to summer pastures. In the fall, they make the same trip in reverse to reach the warmer plains for the winter. Our hearts have gone out to them for years as we see them occasionally in the hospital. Who can reach them with the Good News? Praise the Lord, some have heard, like Pari Jan, and have believed. And how encouraging to meet Wayne and Amy Losey with Wycliffe, who have recently come to work specifically with this unreached people group, to learn their peculiar language, and translate the Word.

Now we pass a gangly camel with a huge load of hay, led by a small boy. Another migrant group is passing, but these folk are Pathans from Afghanistan. Their different identity is revealed by the colorful, full swinging skirts and highly decorated bodices of the women's clothing— a real contract to the drab, worn clothes of the Gujar. They also look to be a stronger race, larger in build and bolder in character. A small child rides atop a pony, along with a baby goat and a couple of chickens.

Here on the plains, wheat harvest is in full swing. We pass field after field of golden grain being cut with the hand sickles of patient harvesters. They squat on the ground, inching their way across the fields as they cut. Others tie the stalks into neat sheaves and stack the bundles in piles to await the small portable threshers. These machines are on hire, being towed from place to place by tractors—a real impediment to traffic! We pass groups of swaying camels, loaded with sheaves being taken to some central threshing floor. What an improvement over the older method of preparing a hard packed mud threshing floor and having the grain trodden out by the feet of oxen going around and around. Then the grain has to be winnowed with wooden forks, allowing the breeze to blow away the chaff. This older, Biblical method is still used farther north in the hilly areas where it is harder to get the equipment and tractors in. What a bucolic harvest scene it is, viewed in the glow of the sun's setting rays. But the workers must not feel bucolic after squatting all day, working in the hot sun. They can't go home to a nice, cool shower at day's end. A fortunate few may have a nearby stream, or a communal water tap to splash in.

We drive on toward Islamabad, nearing the market town of Haripur. As we slow down through the crowded bazaar, the market stalls can be seen piled with heaps of yellow loquats, a rather useless, tasteless fruit consisting mostly of seeds and skin. But that is what is in season at the present time. Later, there will be mounds of green and golden mangos, and piles of oranges and tangerines. A dust storm now develops, swirling dirt, leaves, twigs and plastic bags in the air. We close windows. We stop on the other side of Haripur for all the men to pour out of the bus to say their evening prayers at a wayside mosque. It is hot! I lower the window. Then the raindrops splatter in the dust. As the rain increases, I close the window. We are on our way again and the rain continues for 20 or so miles. The refreshing coolness is welcome, and I am gratified that the driver slows down as the road is a slippery menace from the dust turned to a mud film.

We reach Hassan Abdul, turning east onto the double carriageway leading to Islamabad. The rain ends. I lower my window and turn my attention again to the passing scenery. Increasing industrialization mars the scene, with small businesses, shops and bazaars crowding the road-sides. The driver uses the horn often, warning pedestrians, bicyclists, and hand pulled carts to get out of the way. We pass a small Suzuki van which has overturned. Crowds of people are gathered to see the damage and possibly help the injured. We forge ahead, passing colorfully painted and decorated trucks, piled much too high to be stable. The trucks all have black cloth rags flapping from the bumpers and mirrors, warding off the evil eye. Busses are much overloaded, with men and boys sitting on top and standing on the back bumper clinging to the ladder used for loading baggage onto the roof. As we approach the city, my eyes feast on an occasional blooming lavender jacaranda tree, or a bright yellow cassia. As dusk approaches, we turn onto the new four lane divided highway straight to the capitol city. Picking up speed, our driver pulls into Karachi Company on the dot of 7 p.m. I thank him, getting no acknowledgement. I choose a taxi out of long line, which turns out to be a rattly, rusty, noisy one, but the driver gets me to Shifa Hospital in ten minutes. I go directly to Cindy's room. Her surgery is tomorrow.

ED. NOTE: I had been back in Pakistan working for six weeks at Bach Christian Hospital, when I got word of Cindy's knee injury playing soft-ball at the American Embassy. She had surgery in Pakistan. Two weeks later we returned to the USA, where she had further surgery.

25

Afterword

Since the visit to Pakistan in 1999, we were back again the last three months of 2002. By then, our son Nate and family had had to return to the States because of health reasons, but Cindy was there at the ESL School teaching Afghans. Russ and I both taught at our Zarephath Bible Institute in Rawalpindi, a half hour drive from where we lived with Cindy in Islamabad. It was a joy to be "back home" once again. Then in 2006, we were able to travel to Pakistan for the 50th Anniversary of our Bach Christian Hospital. We were there in 1956 when it first started, so it was a privilege to be there to celebrate 50 years of ministry.

Our daughter Patty and her husband Carl, spent several years as missionaries in the Philippines under the Christian and Missionary Alliance. Then they were 17 years at the headquarters office in Colorado Springs where Carl was Candidate Coordinator and Patty developed the Archives. Now they are pastoring a C&MA church in Lancaster, PA.

Nate is the outreach (missions) pastor at a large church in Indianapolis, and travels to various mission fields as he works to enlarge the missions ministry of his church. We are blessed to be close enough to see his family frequently.

Cindy is still happily engaged in reaching Afghans in Pakistan at the ESL School. God is doing unusual and life changing things through that ministry. If there is a "next book" it will include many of the fascinating stories of Afghan believers she has been able to disciple.

Psalm 96:2-3, "Sing to the Lord, praise his name; proclaim his salvation day by day. DECLARE HIS GLORY AMONG THE NATIONS, his marvelous deeds among all peoples."

About the Author

$\mathcal{P}$hyllis Irwin, M.D., grew up in a small southern Indiana town, a long way from the Northwest Frontier Province in Pakistan where she spent most of her adult life. Challenged in her pre-med years at Asbury College to missionary work abroad, she went on to graduate summa cum laude from Indiana University School of Medicine. She and her husband Russ served 39 years with The Evangelical Alliance Mission. She worked at Bach Christian Hospital, ministering to the medical and spiritual needs of the Muslim populace. Phyllis was for many years the Medical Superintendent of the hospital, retiring in 1995 to live in Noblesville, Indiana. She and her husband continue to be active in their home church and in speaking and teaching opportunities.

LaVergne, TN USA
14 July 2010
189542LV00002B/2/P